Singaporeans think SPGs are little better than prostitutes. Expatriates disagree. They think she is a lot better. She's free.

THE OFFICIAL GUIDE TO THE

SARONG PARTY GIRL

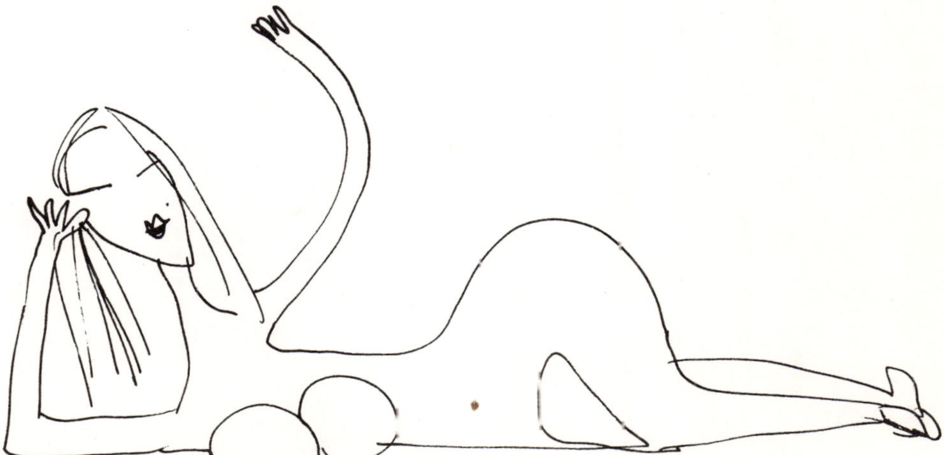

RECLINING NUDE

THE OFFICIAL GUIDE TO THE

SARONG PARTY GIRL

JIM **AITCHISON**

ILLUSTRATED BY

THESEUS **CHAN**

Angsana Books
SINGAPORE

The characters portrayed in this book bear no resemblance to any persons, living or dead, or just having a good time.

Published by Angsana Books

Angsana Books is an imprint of
FLAME OF THE FOREST Pte Ltd
Yishun Industrial Park A
Blk 1003, #02-432
Singapore 2776
Tel: 7532071

Cover by Theseus Chan and Mangosteen Designs

Printed in Singapore

ISBN 981-3056-36-3

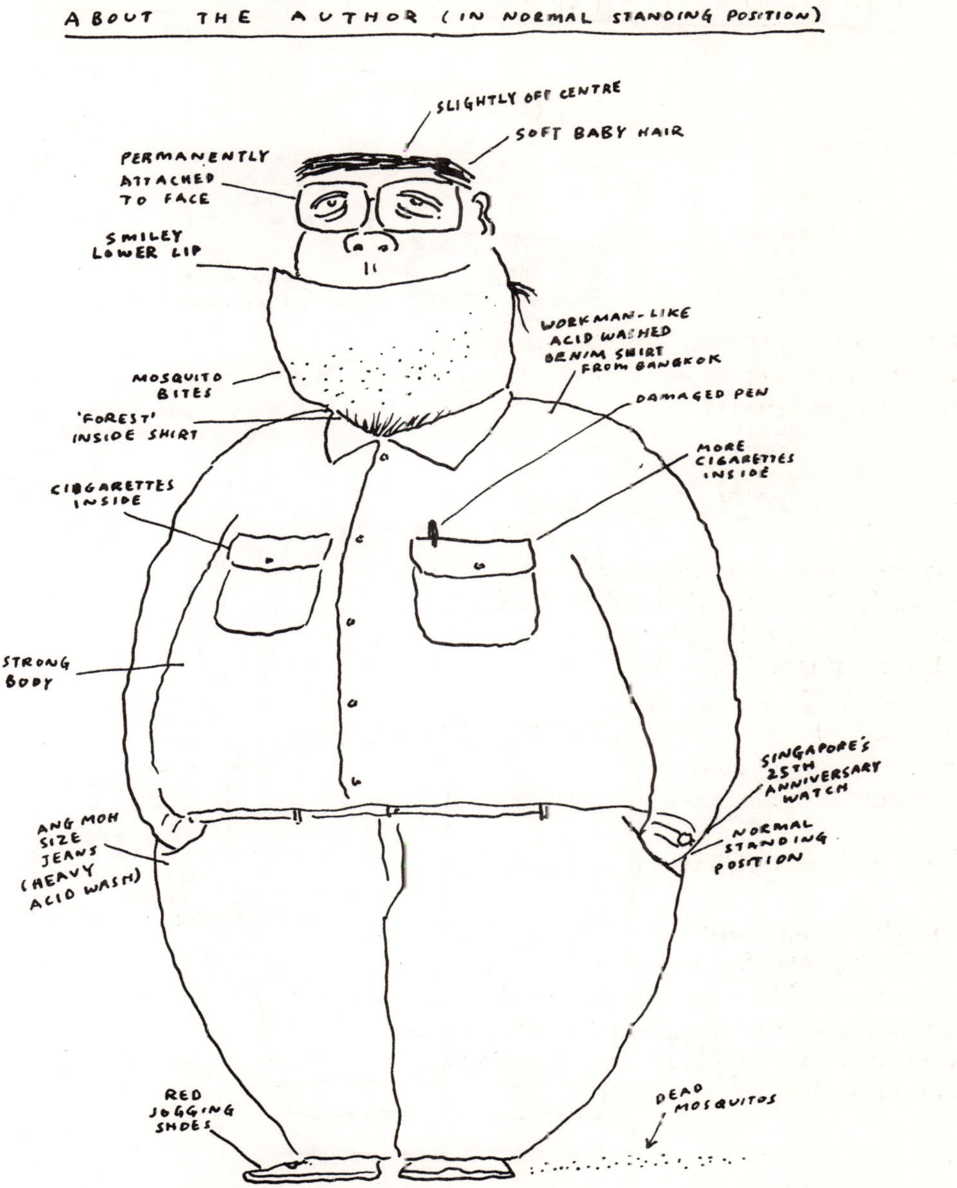

This is Jim. He knows SPGs well. Jim is big in size. Very big.

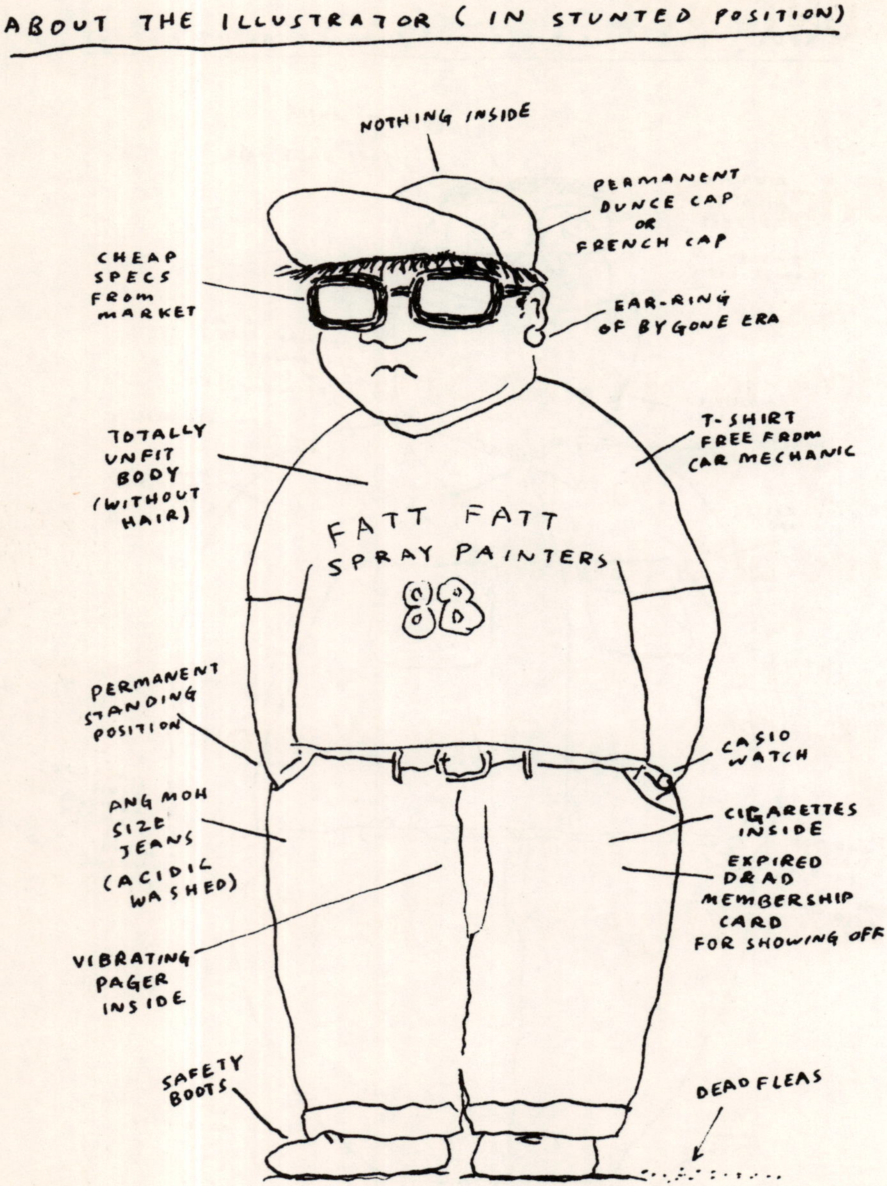

And this is Theseus. He's small. But not so small, lah!

CONTENTS

CHAPTER 1

ORIGIN OF THE SPG

The Sarong Party Girl (SPG) is believed to have first appeared in the last days of British imperialism. She was attracted to Officers' Balls in the 1920s.

Her sarong was worn as a signal that she could be disrobed and ready for action in seconds.

At one stage, there was even talk of the British army raising a regiment of SPGs. However, it did not get off the ground. Just as well. It would have been the first to surrender.

There have been many derivatives of the SPG. Once there were Chinese Taxi Girls who wore cheong-sams. Then came Satay Party Girls: satay

being a piece of meat on a long stick. Recently, there's been a rash of Sari Party Girls, constantly in demand by German expatriates.

THE SPECIES

There's something in the way the SPG moves, a bit like a little girl wearing her mother's shoes. A faintly amateurish attempt to look provocative and sexy, which isn't actually necessary. You see, most SPGs are attractive. And provocative. And sexy. And therein lies the problem.

Why do these pretty girls force themselves to be noticed, much to the amusement of everyone watching?

Why have they got "Look at me!" written all over them?

The truth is, she is sending out desperate radar signals to expatriates. By wiggling her figure, over-emphasising her long legs with skimpy shorts and flashing her eyes eagerly, she is trying to turn every opportunity of impressing an expatriate into the "beginning of a meaningful relationship". Meaningful to her, that is.

If a white man scoops her up into his glamourous world of partying, fast cars, Studebaker's, and expatriate salaries, then all her efforts have been worth it.

CAN I BUY
YOU A DRINK?
YES.

Once there has been one white man, there will be more.

It's not that she is a nymphomaniac, rather that she is hell bent on associating with expatriates at any cost.

She soon learns that expatriates will discard her, in time, in favour of another SPG. She accepts this fact, almost without resentment. So, once she has one relationship established, she is constantly on the watch for the next.

Strangely enough, she is happy just being admitted to the world of the expatriate. Once there, she will look after her own interests.

Her sister SPGs will share a similar outlook. In one sense, they are in deadly competition with each other. Yet, on the other hand, they can recognise each

other's needs. In the same way that the expatriate will swap notes on the SPGs they've notched up, the SPGs will do the same. They can compare experiences, discuss triumphs and failures, and be rather fatalistic about the whole thing.

SPGs do not see themselves as tarts; neither do they perceive themselves as hookers.

NOT ALL SPG LIKE ANG MOHS

SPGs have a genuine need to be accepted by expatriates, to have relationships with them, and to flit from one to the other.

SPGs are also aware of their place in Singapore society. Frankly, they despise it. If other women are critical of their behaviour, or if Singapore men take shots at them, it is of no importance. By being an SPG, she has cast off from the herd. In her book, Singapore has little to offer. She sees the Singaporean way of life as limited and boring. She has discovered an alternative; a cosmopolitan, Western way of living, where freedom and lack of inhibition rule. But she is sadly wrong. Because in the West, as in the East, strong social values are still the order of the day when it comes to settling down and starting a family.

The fact that she uses sex as her vehicle to gain that new lifestyle is no big deal to her. She is a healthy young woman, and sex is a perfectly natural drive.

Sadly though, there's a price. She will soon become a rather shallow stereotype, and those around her will lose sight of the real woman.

PREFERENCES FOR MEN ARE ALREADY HIGHLY DEVELOPED AT A YOUNG AGE.

ATLAS *A handy reference guide so that an SPG can at least locate the country of the man she slept with the night before.*

Why do expatriates pursue her? Well, for one thing, she makes herself easily available. Imagine yourself a stranger in a strange country. Along comes an SPG: she represents the most immediately available form of female companionship.

And, of course, she is the embodiment of the male Caucasian dream: the exotic, erotic Oriental girl, Suzie Wong in a sarong, complete with flashing eyes, a sexy figure and a sexually alert personality. She is the girl he dreamed of finding in the East!

Tragically for her, she will often be the first local girl an expatriate meets. But there it will stop. Most single expatriates will be either transferred to another country, or will settle down with a real local girl: the kind of girl with the same values that they would marry back home. In fact, as more expatriates and Singapore girls marry, the SPG will become even more of an anachronism. She will be left to pursue yet another white man, and another, and another.

Does this make our SPG a tart? Some would say "yes", but consider the facts. Her upbringing was probably quite strict and it's not unnatural for a healthy young girl to rebel a little. She has picked up enough English language skills to be comfortable talking to expatriates. And, above all else, she sees a chance to elevate her social status. Or so she thinks.

Wouldn't SPGs be better off marrying local boys?

Well, if you took such things as money, material possessions and future security into account, yes.

ANG MOH HAVING A SLAM DUNK

But they're not part of the SPG agenda. Her objective, initially, is to discover herself. And to relate herself to an expatriate lifestyle.

SPG SISTERS – THE TRAITS RUN IN THE FAMILY

In her view, local boys are far too limited in outlook. She has made a mental leap into another dimension, and where the mind goes the body is sure to follow.

She genuinely believes that expatriates have more to offer: socially, financially and even culturally.

SPGs ARE UPDATED WITH THE LATEST FASHION TRENDS. THIS IS THE WAIF LOOK

Maybe she has had one or two local boyfriends, but once she has stepped into the expatriate world, there can be no turning back. Her parents will obviously be shocked to see their teenaged daughter in the company of forty-year-old expatriates. Or even men older than her father! They can, of course, disown her – but that's not the Singaporean way. They may try to reason with her, but chances are they wil accept things as they are. And pray that she will find her happiness eventually.

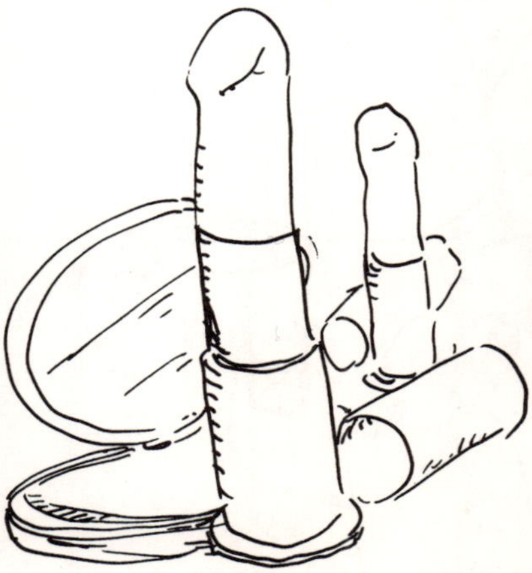

SPGS BASIC MAKE UP KIT

The most vocal objections will come from her relatives, especially the older generation.

Is she ashamed of being Asian perhaps? Some think so. They might even say she has closed the door on her own culture before she has really opened the door on another.

Caught in the middle, she is neither Asian nor Western. Or does her outrageous behaviour merely conceal her insecurity?

SPG DEVELOPS TALENT AT A TENDER AGE

And the more tongues wag, the more the SPG wiggles. Public opinion is not a problem to her.

Is there such a thing as an old SPG?

Yes. If one accepts old as being 30 to 35.

The SPG will work her way through a progression of Caucasian males until she reaches her mid-twenties. By that time, she is probably ready to settle down, but – alas – she will have been labelled an "easy lay". Catching an expatriate husband will be virtually impossible. So she will probably go overseas for a few years. To work. To experience Western culture first-hand. And to enjoy more Caucasian male companionship.

If she's lucky – very lucky – she may find true love overseas. In London, or Paris, or Los Angeles. Or, more likely, in Manchester, or Glasgow, or White Plains, New York.

Most likely, though, she'll return home to Singapore...

and reappear at Brannigans.

She'll be a sadder but wiser girl, a touch heavier around the hips. And she'll continue as before: bed-hopping her way through the expat community, perhaps a little more wearily and warily, and asking for a more responsible relationship.

SPG WITH EXPAT FROM TAXI DRIVER'S POINT OF VIEW

And she'll have more character. She'll have more discernment. And she'll spend more time at home, minding her pet cat or dog.

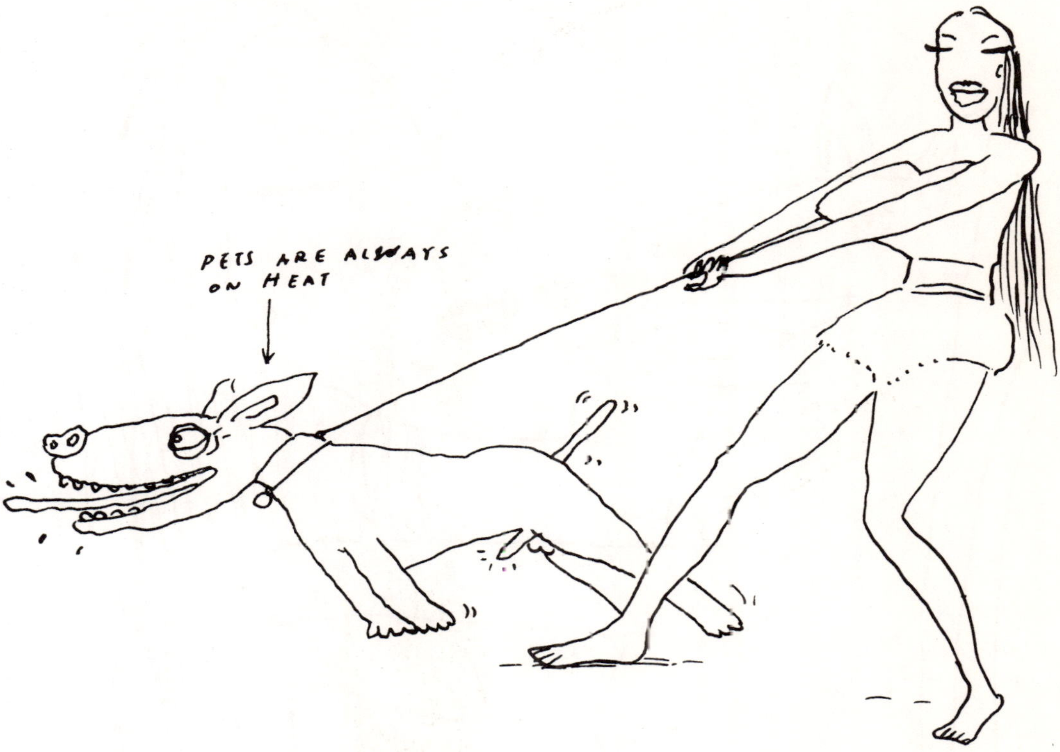

100 PLUS *This does not refer to an isotonic drink, but the number of men an SPG consumes every month.*

But she will still be, deep down, an SPG.

CHAPTER 2

HOW TO SPOT AN SPG

An SPG gives herself away the minute she opens her mouth. She speaks with a "kentang" accent. Whether or not she practises her accent by inserting a real potato in her mouth, nobody really knows.

But if she can't find one, there will always be an expatriate nearby, ready to help.

OINK *The loudest sound made by an SPG.*

SPG – AN ALL-OVER VIEW IDENTIFIER

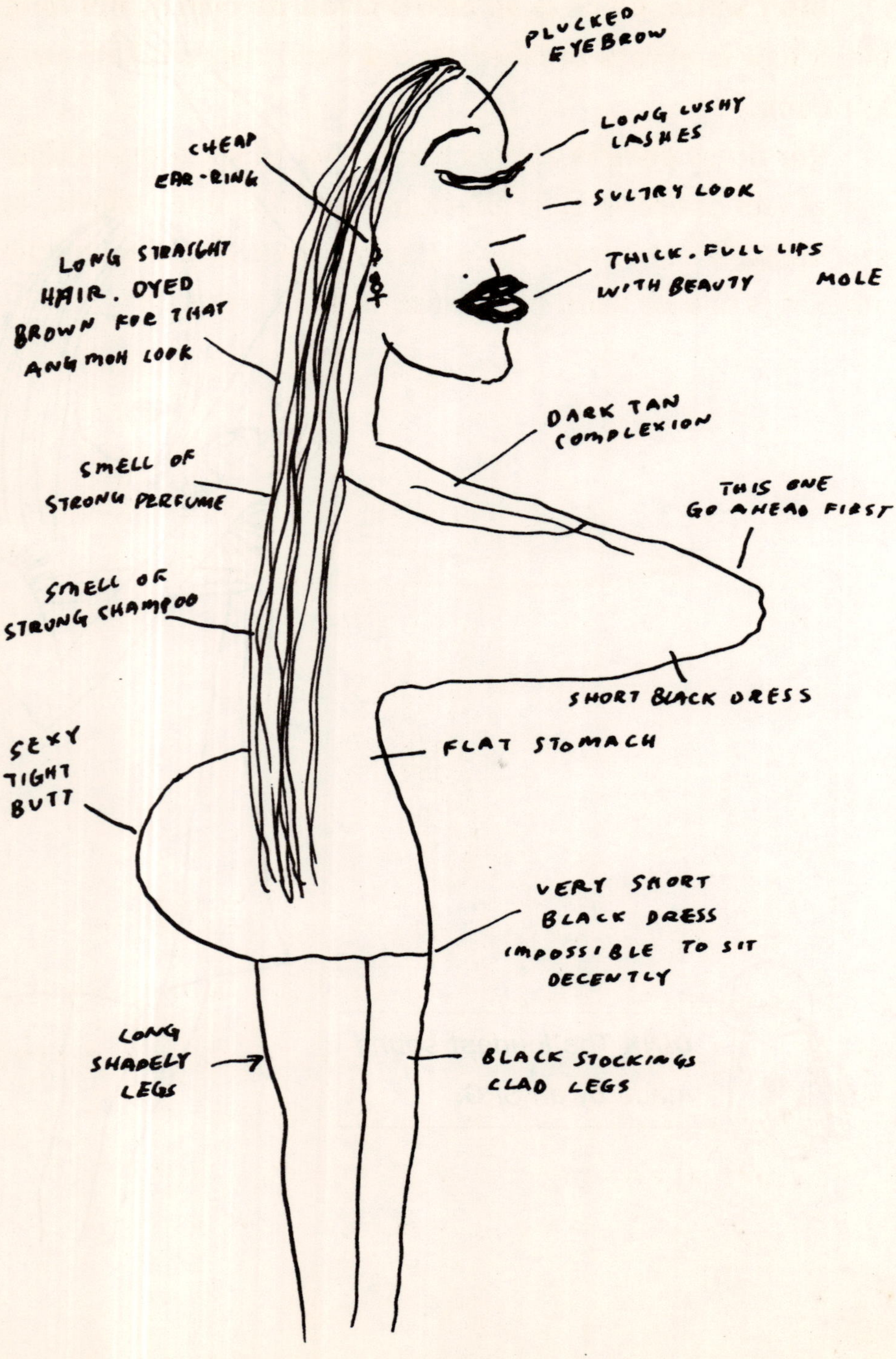

After white, black is an SPG's favourite colour. Her long black hair is always brushed straight and reaches half way down her back.

Her dress code is always black, too. Black dresses that reveal lots of brown skin. Black mini-skirts, black shorts, black stockings. Black is not only a classy colour, but black undies and stockings can be worn for a week without washing.

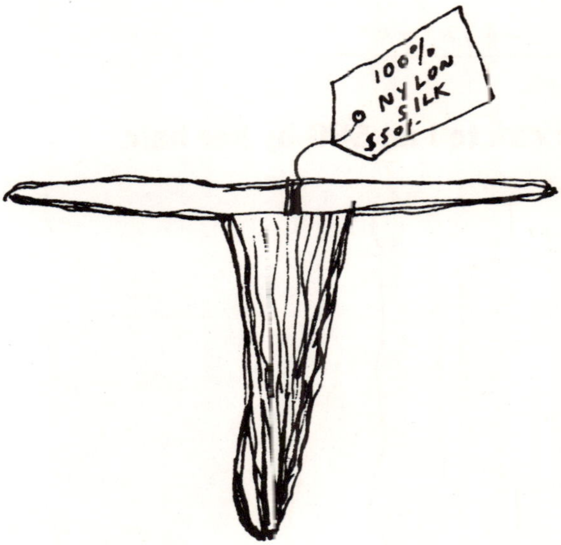

SPGs PRIDE THEMSELVES WITH
THEIR KNOWLEGDE OF UNDERWEAR
G-STRINGS IS A OBVIOUS FAVOURITE.
DEFINITELY A HIT WITH THEM
AS A PRESENT. A SIGN THAT
YOU CARE ABOUT HER.

You can tell when an SPG has done her washing...

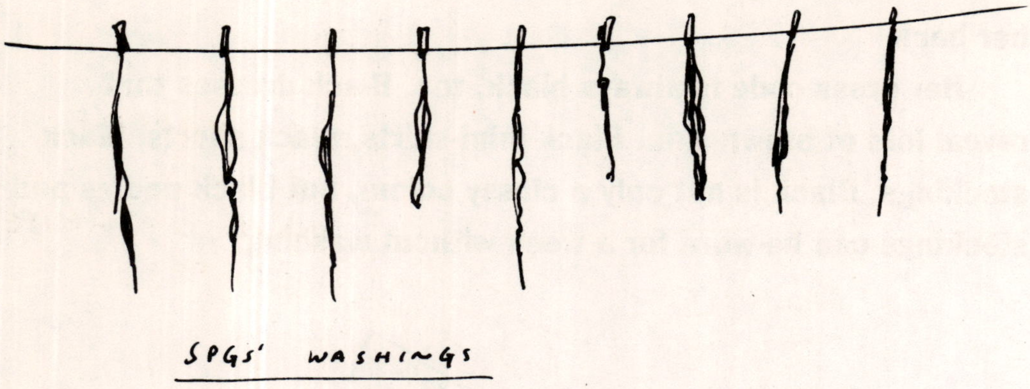

...just as you can tell an SPG by her hair.

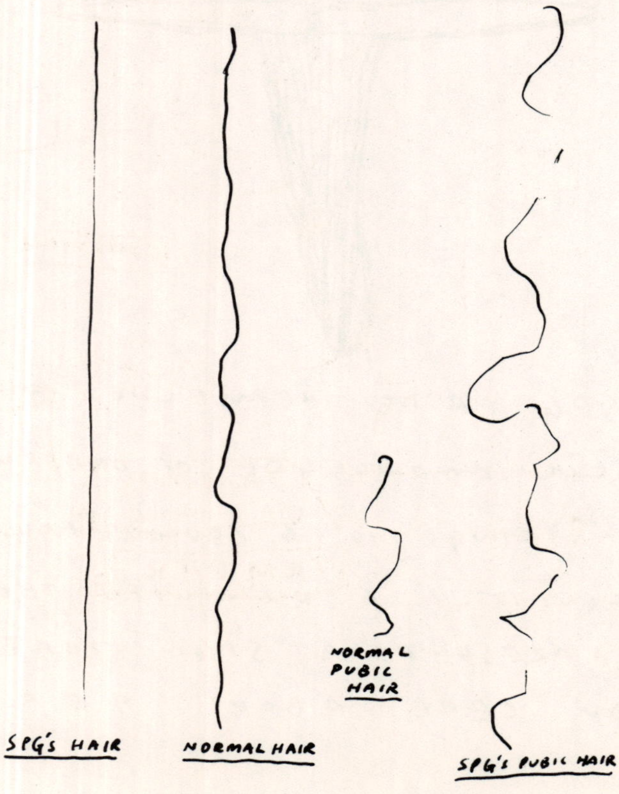

98% of all SPGs wear black bras. The average SPG buys two new bras a week. The average SPG loses two new bras a week.

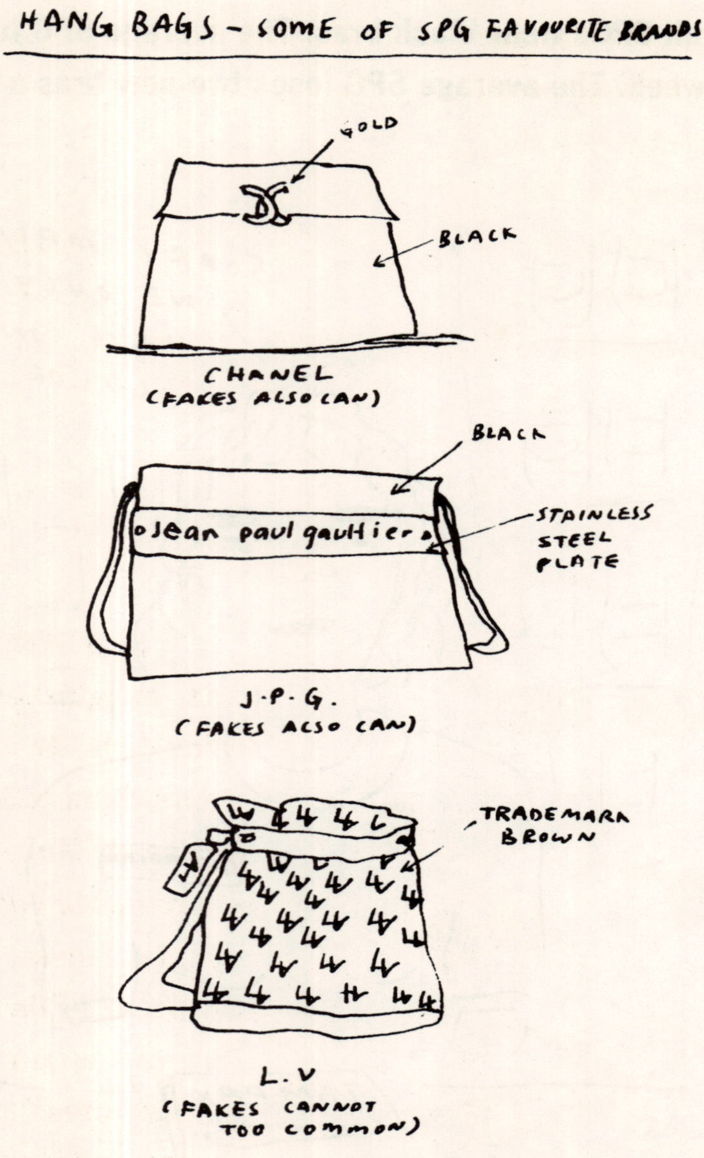

SPGs are mindful of the accessories they use. Handbags, shoes, eyewear, they have a distinctive flavour — they are all expensive.

SPGs wear the highest-healed shoes in Singapore in order to exaggerate the length and shape of their legs. Precariously high heels ensure that when an SPG walks, everything moves.

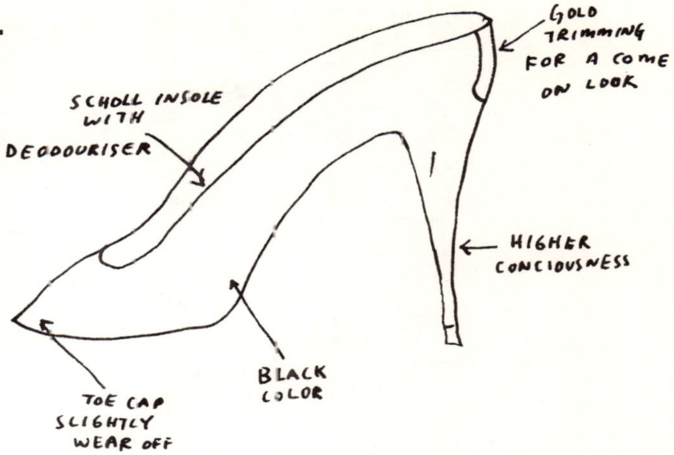

A TYPICAL SPG SHOE

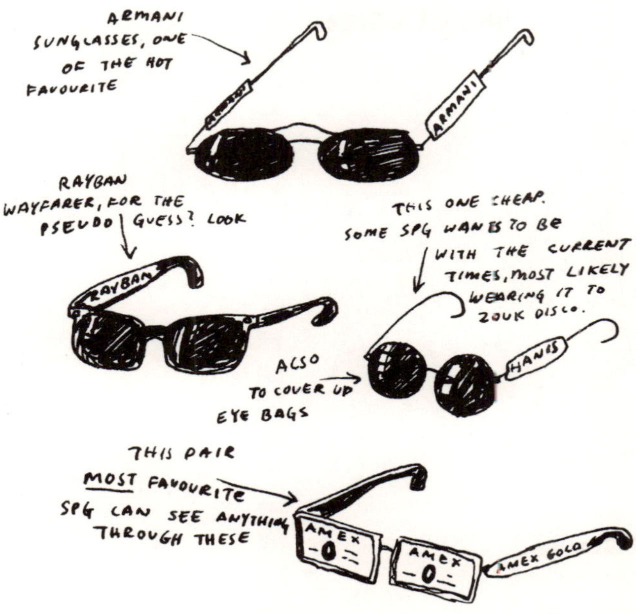

SUNGLASSES ARE SPG ESSENTIAL ACCESSORY, THEY ARE EASY COVER-UP ESPECIALLY WHEN BARGAINING WITH THE CHINA TOWN HAWKER. WHEN THE NEED ARISES, MAKE MAN TALLER, DARKER & HANDSOMER.

A true SPG will always wear sunglasses, even on rainy days. At night, she wears them pushed back on her head. Many SPGs are short-sighted and wear contact lenses. However, 98.8% of SPGs have perfect long distance vision so they can spy credit cards in dark discos and identify an expat male at a distance of over 15,000 metres.

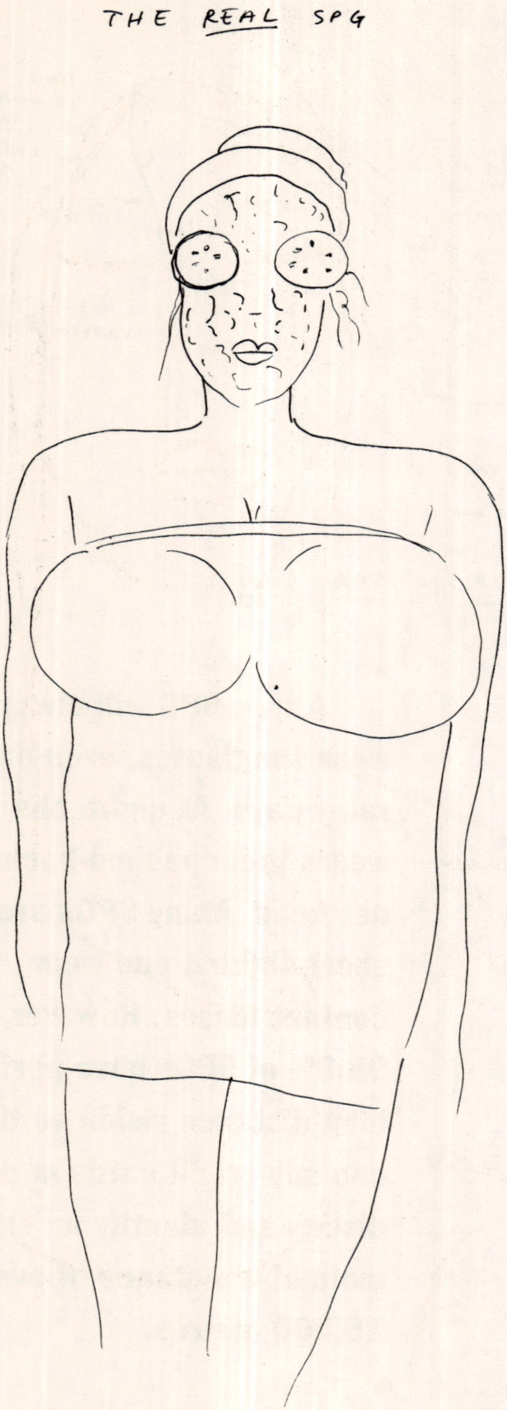

This is what an SPG looks like at home.

This is what an SPG looks like when she leaves home.

SPGs are famous for their breasts. Most have developed a 36-inch breast by the age of 15.

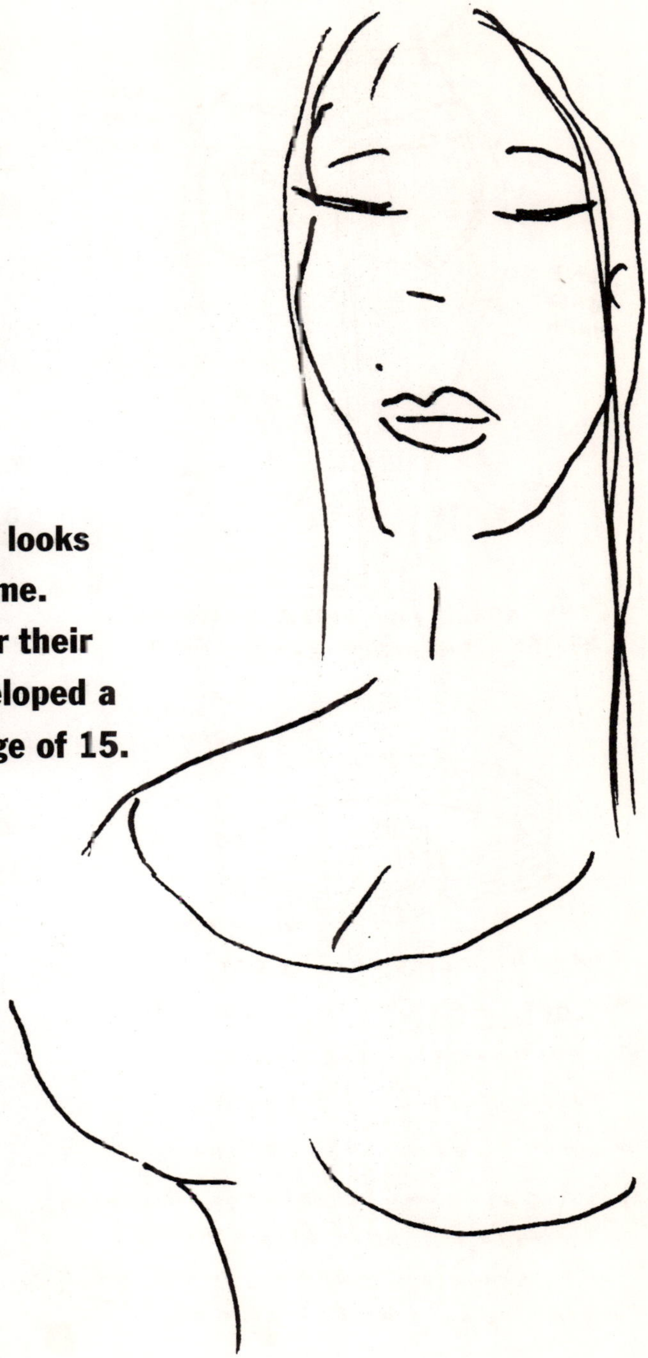

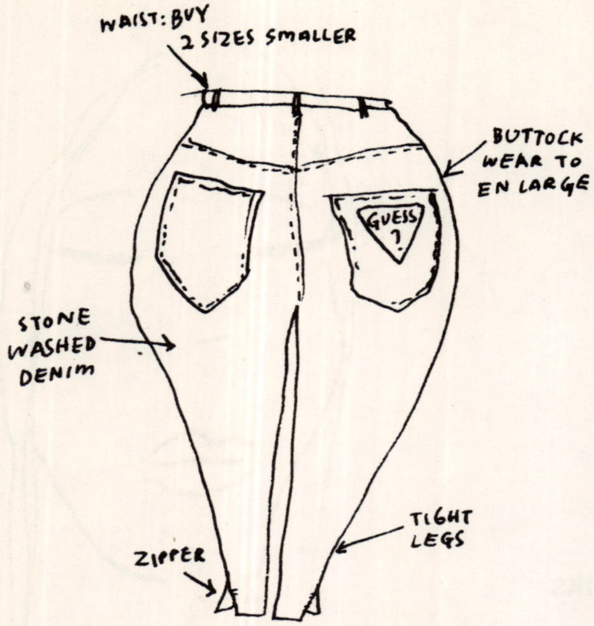

JEANS ARE SPG OTHER FAVOURITE ATTIRE. FAVOURITE BRAND: GUESS?

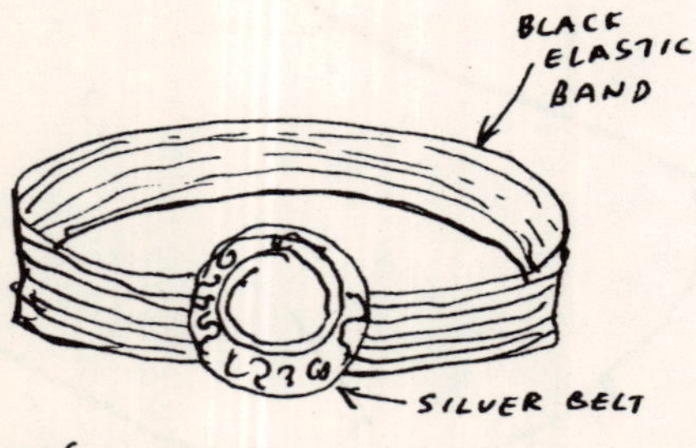

STRONG ELASTIC BELT IS A HOT FAVOURITE WITH SPGS. IT ENHANCES THE SMALL WAIST EVEN FURTHER. MOSTLY WORN WITH TIGHTS & TIGHT LONG SLEEVE TRANSPARENT T-SHIRTS. SPG LIKE THINGS TIGHT BECAUSE CERTAIN PARTS OF THEIR BODY ARE LOOSE.

They are also noted for tight, trim bottoms which are approximately the size of a white man's hands.

SPGs detest having child-bearing hips. Most have the hips of a 12-year-old boy, which is very appropriate because they also have the brains of a 12-year-old boy.

Genuine SPGs will have very tanned skin. However, to avoid overexposure to the sun, it is recommended that a white man's body be placed over the SPG's to prevent damage.

SPG SPEND QUITE A SUBSTANTIAL AMOUNT OF MONEY ON SHAMPOO

Another reason why SPGs spend so much time tanning their legs is to cover all traces of varicose veins.

Over 85% of all SPGs have to shave their armpits more than once a day. Many have short fingernails, too, so they can count money faster. Their feet are always perfectly manicured and an SPG's toes are remarkably agile and can perform many functions.

Sadly only 23% of SPGs still wear sarongs. Older SPGs, in their forties and fifties, still wear sarongs to bed.

DENTAL CARE - SPG STYLE

By now, of course, you probably think it will be quite easy to spot an SPG.

Wrong.

There are countless thousands of girls in Singapore who wear black, and have long legs, and prefer Western culture, and have expatriate friends.

You see, girls who are SPGs have to be SPGs in their minds.

CHAPTER 3

THE SPG AND MEN

At the sight of white flesh, the SPG unleashes all her charms. And flattery will get her everywhere.

The white man relishes her attention. Even the most cynical veteran enters each new affair with renewed lust and vigour. Some even believe that the Chinese name Tan was derived from the colour of her skin. Virtually every SPG's slim, lithe body is stroked with a deep, glowing tan. Is half her income spent on Coppertone? Who knows. But one thing is for sure: SPGs believe their bodies are their temples, which is why they worship them so often. And happily invite white men to worship in them, too.

Her sexuality could well be nothing more than a thin veneer over a materialistic soul, a kampong girl with dollar signs in her eyes. But given a choice, she will take a white man over a local man any day.

HI, HANDSOME, YOU WANT GOOD TIME?

SPGs regard local men as inferior wimps who can only offer a lifetime of boredom in an HDB flat.

A true SPG would never go out with an Ah Beng. She cringes at the thought of travelling in a Nissan pickup with a man who perms his hair. She also detests local businessmen because they only use their mouths to talk about themselves.

DANCES WITH WOLVES *A movie about an SPG at Studebakers.*

If a local girl wants you to kiss her on both cheeks, she's pretentious. If she wants you to kiss her on both cheeks and then stand up and kiss her on the lips, she's an SPG.

On the other hand, local men aged 45 to 65 despise SPGs, or any girl for that matter who associates with white expatriate males.

However, young local men have absolutely no objection to SPGs because they keep white men away from higher class, attractive girls.

Of course, once a local girl becomes an SPG, local pressure forces her to become even more Westernised. She can no longer call into a provision shop because the owner's wife won't talk to her.

CULTRAL DIFFERENCES BETWEEN SPG & JAPANESE MEN IS EASILY MISUNDERSTOOD

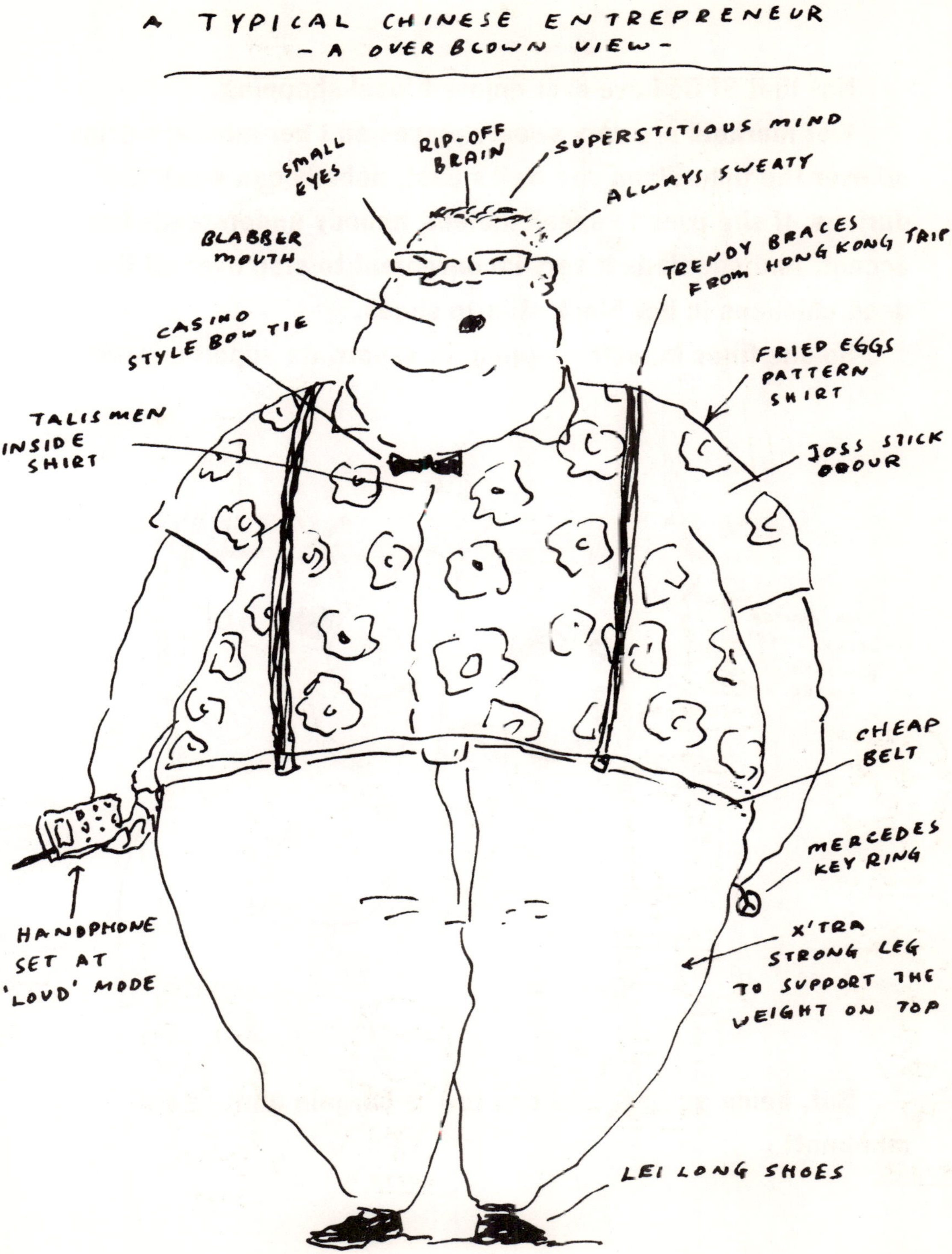
A TYPICAL CHINESE ENTREPRENEUR
- A OVER BLOWN VIEW -
SMALL EYES
RIP-OFF BRAIN
SUPERSTITIOUS MIND
ALWAYS SWEATY
BLABBER MOUTH
TRENDY BRACES FROM HONG KONG TRIP
CASINO STYLE BOW TIE
FRIED EGGS PATTERN SHIRT
TALISMEN INSIDE SHIRT
JOSS STICK ODOUR
CHEAP BELT
MERCEDES KEY RING
HANDPHONE SET AT 'LOUD' MODE
X'TRA STRONG LEG TO SUPPORT THE WEIGHT ON TOP
LEI LONG SHOES

Not that SPGs have ever enjoyed local shopping.

Wet markets are very sweaty places and her mascara drips all over the fish. When she walks past, nobody can smell the durians. If she tries to speak dialect, nobody understands her accent. And she finds it very inconvenient to step over all the dead chickens in her black stiletto shoes.

So she finds herself shopping in expatriate supermarkets.

But, being an SPG, she can turn a bargain hunt into a manhunt!

SPGs wearing sunglasses and fringed denim shorts can frequently be found loitering by the cheese cabinets or seeking the advice of single expatriate males in the wine section.

One supermarket in District 11 serves more SPGs than any other supermarket in Singapore. It is also the only shop in Singapore where less than 5% of female customers wear bras.

LARGE
LARGE
LARGE
*$!?$, WHERE IS THE LARGE SIZE?
MEDIUM
MEDIUM
SMALL
SMALL

No SPGs shop at People's Park. Instead she will go to Holland Village in very daring shorts cut-away sharply at the bottom.

And she will never, never take part in Lucky Draws, believing them to be too undignified and Chinak. Besides, she also has great difficulty remembering her I.C. number.

Any expatriate crazy enough to take an SPG shopping will be bled white.

In a seemingly illogical foray through the fashion department, she will buy dozens of things which she doesn't need (but her mother does).

When she puts her hand in an expatriate's pocket, he is sure to feel a rather numbing sensation.

According to SPG mythology, she welcomes any excuse to jump into bed with a white man.

Obviously, this is not always the case, and SPGs have developed many plausible excuses to rid themselves of unwanted whites.

The most commonly used are:

1. Have to go toilet
2. Have to go temple
3. Have to go mother house
4. Have to go shopping, loh!
5. My aunty dying one
6. Got wedding
7. Got headache
8. Got flu
9. Got heavy flow
10. Got stomach cramps
11. Got wind
12. Got gastric
13. Got diarrhoea
14. Got cramps, wind, gastric and diarrhoea.

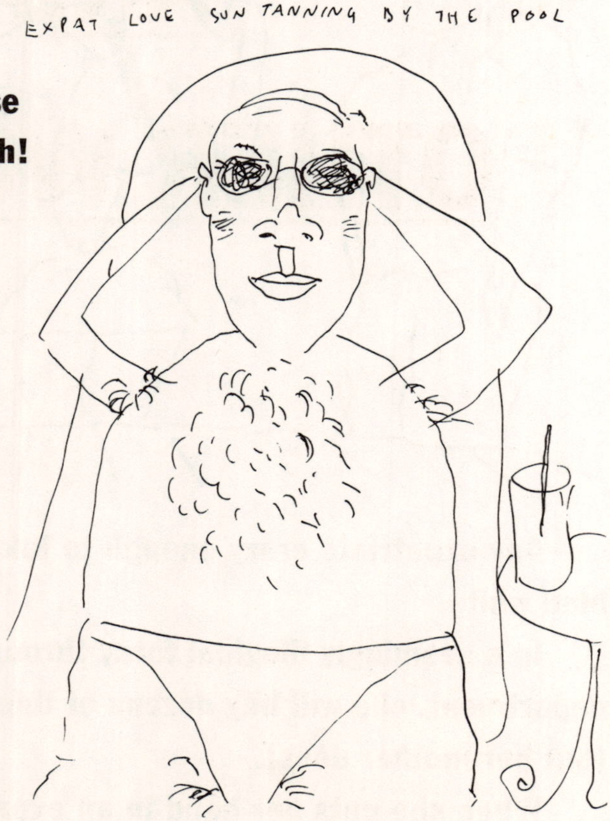

CHAPTER 4

THE SPG AND OTHER WOMEN

The SPG has a vast number of natural enemies including expatriate wives. It appears she is a threat to them all, but rather than sharpen their acts, they sharpen their knives.

Her nubile body is the envy of rich tai-tais. They would never dare to make love in a room with the lights on. The SPG is unrepressed. She doesn't care if the lights are on and the blinds are up. In fact, she doesn't much care about having a room in the first place.

YOUNG TAI-TAI WAITING FOR AHMAD* AT PROMENADE

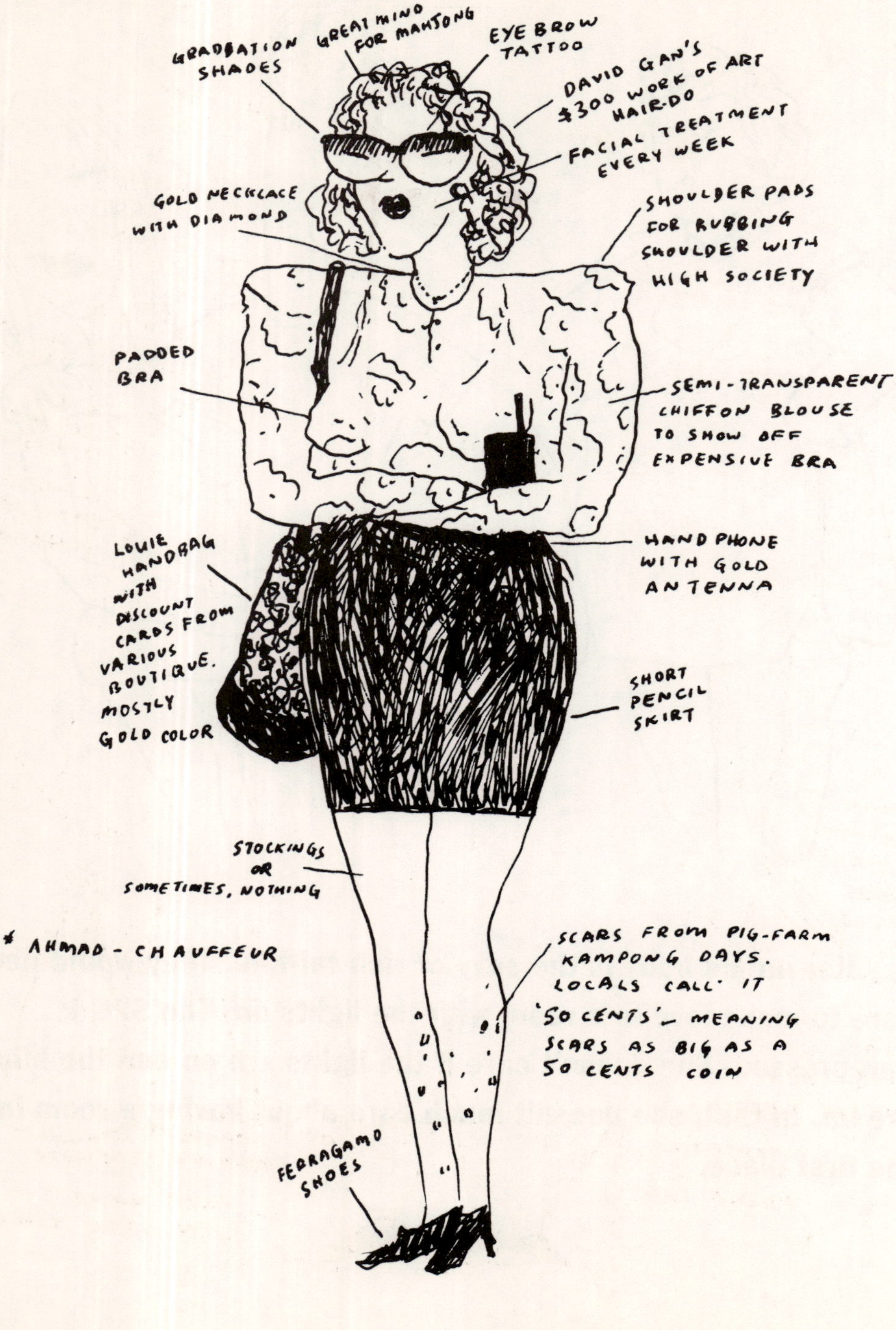

A TYPICAL CHINESE ENTREPRENEUR'S MISSUS

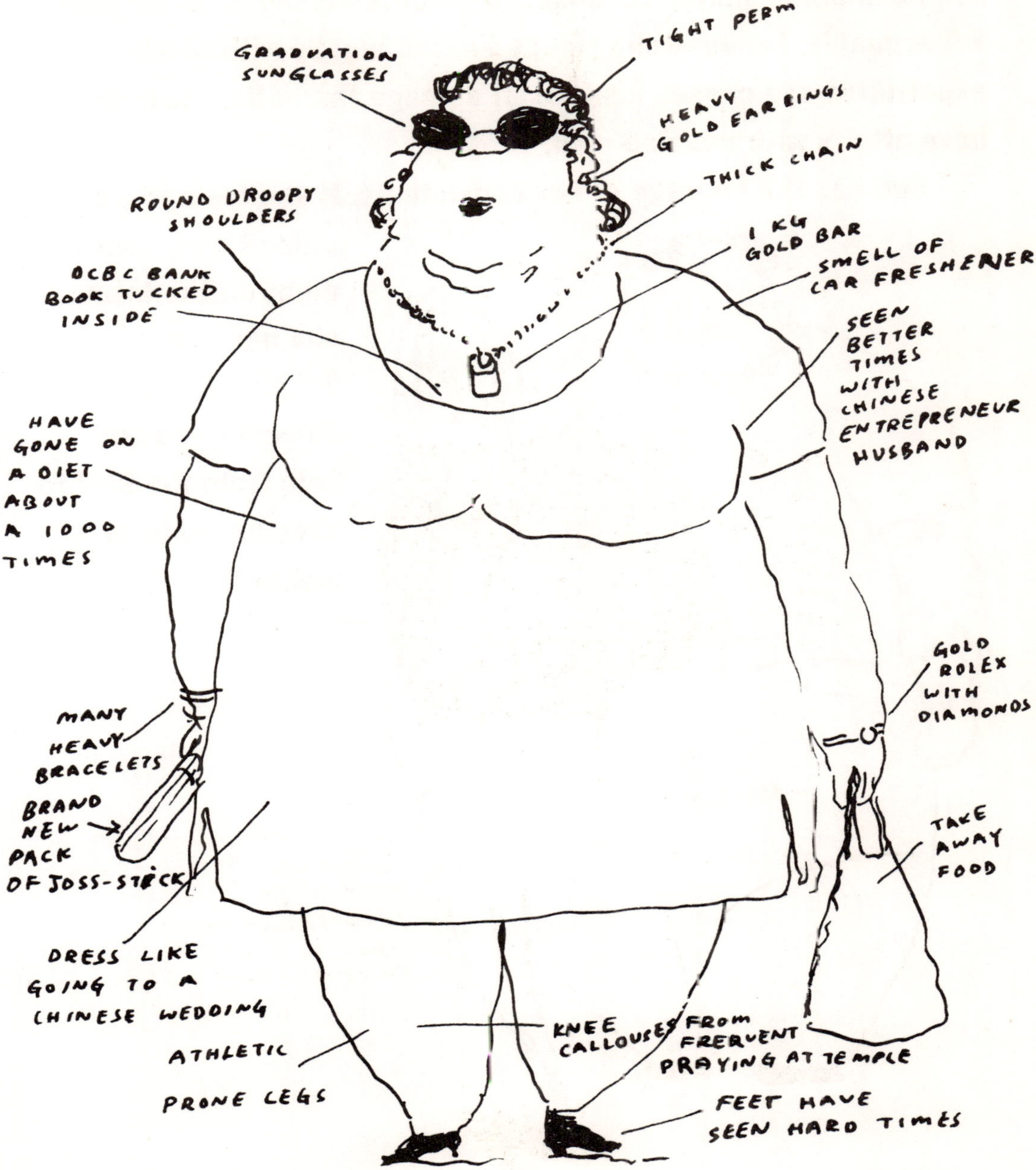

The SPG is branded as an exhibitionist, a slut and a nymphomaniac simply because she flaunts herself at white men. Yet arguably, because she sleeps around mostly with single expatriates she causes less social damage than other girls who have affairs with married men.

She has the courage of her convictions. If she feels like an uninhibited, sleazy night on the town, she has one.

She certainly doesn't need any help from the SDU to obey her natural instincts.

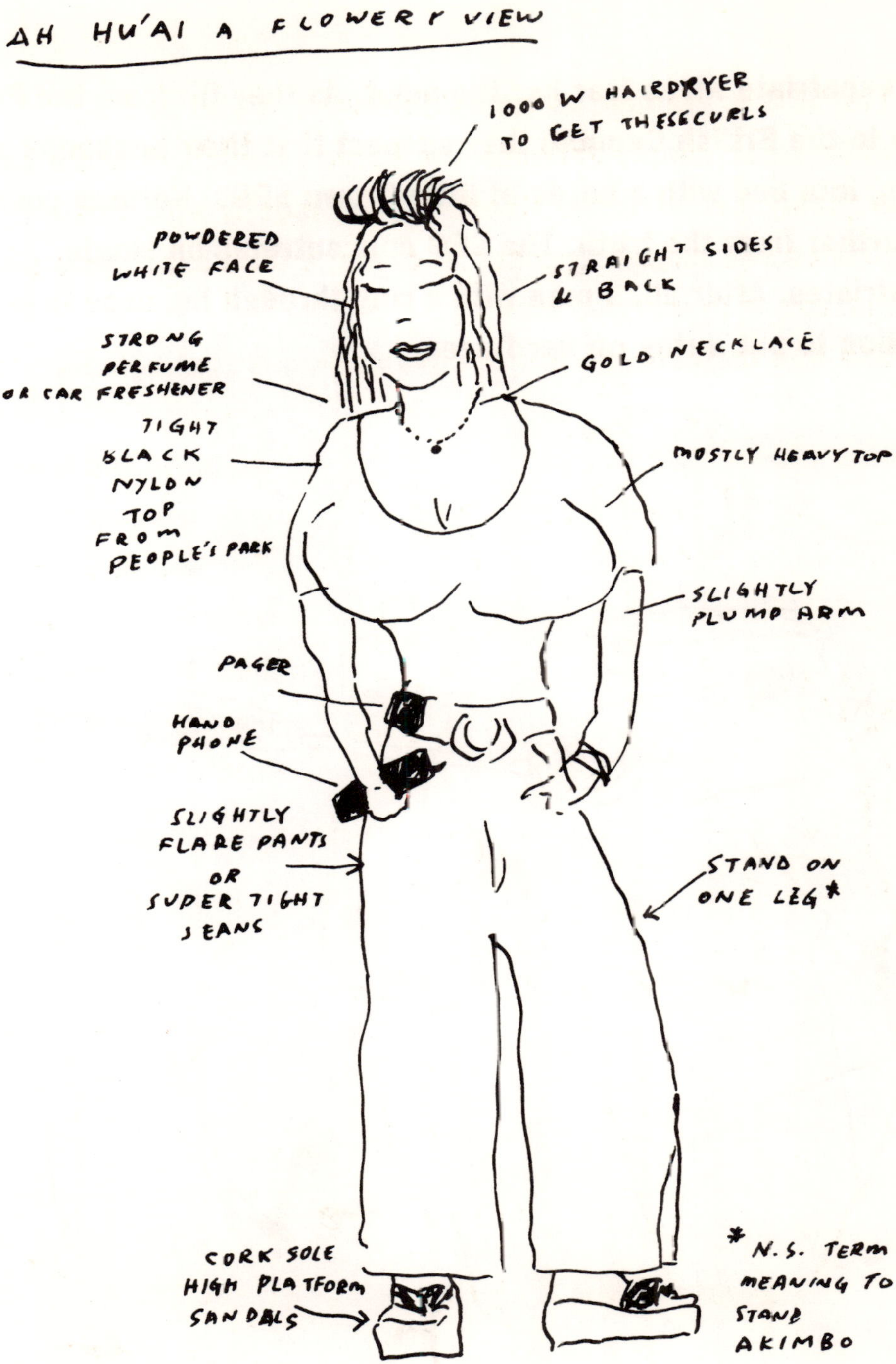
AH HU'AI A FLOWERY VIEW
1000 W HAIRDRYER TO GET THESE CURLS
POWDERED WHITE FACE
STRAIGHT SIDES & BACK
STRONG PERFUME OR CAR FRESHENER
GOLD NECKLACE
TIGHT BLACK NYLON TOP FROM PEOPLE'S PARK
MOSTLY HEAVY TOP
SLIGHTLY PLUMP ARM
PAGER
HAND PHONE
SLIGHTLY FLARE PANTS OR SUPER TIGHT JEANS
STAND ON ONE LEG*
CORK SOLE HIGH PLATFORM SANDALS
* N.S. TERM MEANING TO STAND AKIMBO

Expatriate wives fear her the most. As they flit from the Polo Club to the British Council, they suspect that their husbands are diving into bed with a horde of little brown SPGs. Nothing could be further from the truth. The SPG concentrates on single expatriates. After all, a man with a ring through his nose is in no position to put a ring on her finger.

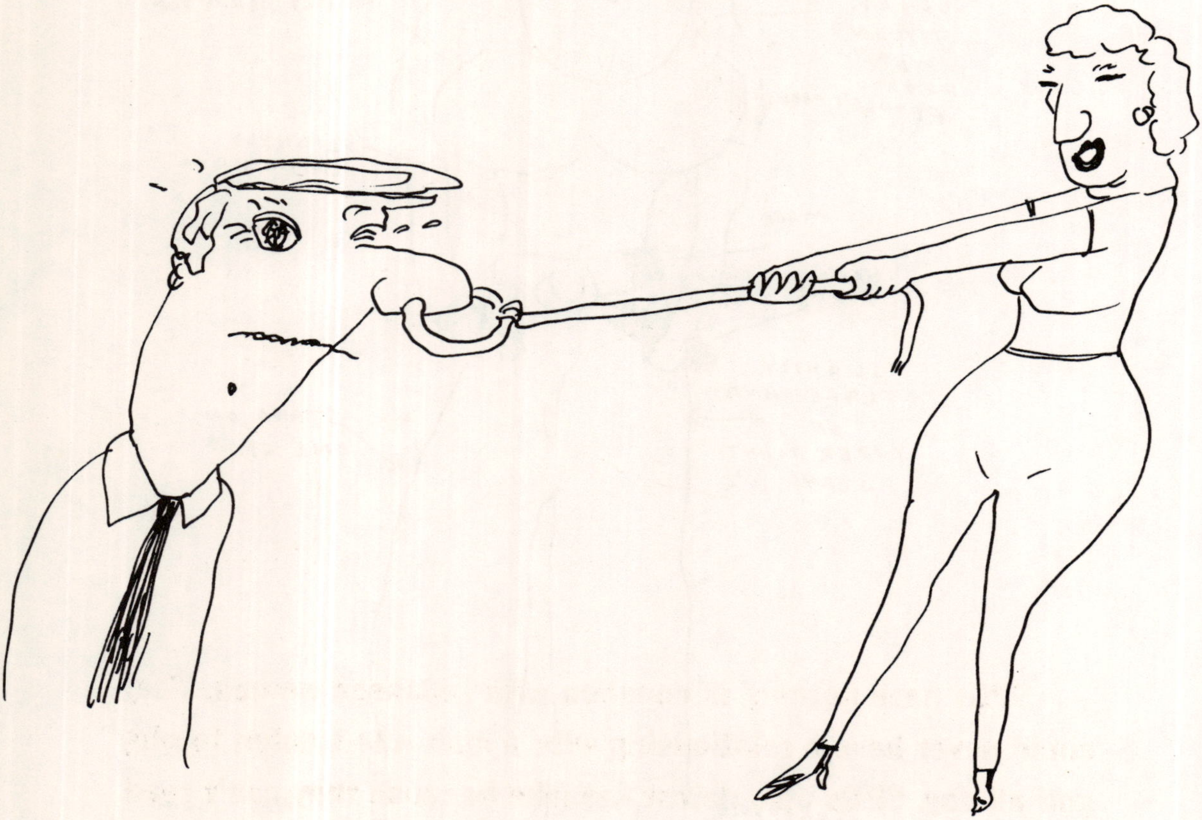

The SPG sees herself as a totally liberated woman. Worldly and sophisticated. An international jetsetter giddily speeding by NTUC Comfort Nissan Cedric from Toa Payoh to Orchard Road.

SPGs have nothing in common with Japanese women. They could never have a relationship with a man who wanted to play golf all day. SPGs also detest karaoke because they can't read the words fast enough.

SPG MOSTLY WALK AROUND NAKED AT HOME. MEMBERS OF THE PUBLIC OFTEN REPORT THESE INCIDENCES TO THE NEWSPAPER.

FLIP FLOPS *Not to be confused with shoes. This is the sound a 40-year-old SPG makes when dancing.*

CHAPTER 5

SCHOOLDAYS WITH THE SPG

In order to sound innocent, a lot of SPGs falsely claim they went to convent schools. And the time spent on their knees in the convent will prove very useful when they mix with white men. Not so.

14 YEAR OLD SPG IN THE MAKING

16 YEAR OLD SPG MAKING SUGGESTIONS

Some Singapore schools are famous for having very short uniforms. Hemlines reach no lower than halfway down the thighs of its pupils (when standing). These young SPGs create havoc at the neighbourhood bus stops by sitting on the railings with their feet apart, directly facing the oncoming traffic. Multiple pile-ups frequently occur.

On sports days, when the young, full-breasted SPGs compete in races, their teachers are deafened by the boing-boing-boing sound.

SPG AFTER SCHOOL

Some students will even have discreet tattoos on their necks, breasts or further down. An erotic tattoo on the inside thigh is regarded as highly sophisticated by the girls, and a very odd birthmark by their teachers.

SPGs struggle with English all their lives. Typical of them will be phrases such as "Can I hept you?" and "Why so big one, lah?"

Many SPGs are the daughters of bus drivers. This explains why they can make so many pick ups in such a short space of time. It also explains why they are so pushy and how they can remain so ignorant of public opinion.

Kampong girls also become SPGs. Their Lim Chu Kang heritage explains the strange grunting noises they make during intercourse. It also explains why they like scraps and trash. Miraculously these girls will have managed to avoid ugly mosquito bites and fifty cent pieces from their kampong days.

SOME SPGS WERE RAISED ON PIG FARMS

Not surprisingly, 88% of all parents do not approve of their daughters becoming SPGs. When an SPG brings her expatriate boyfriend home for dinner, 63% of all parents are shocked, 10% will ban all future visits, 5% send their daughter for psychiatric advice. On the other hand, some will approve of such relationships. And 2% will actually ask the ang moh for a loan.

How can you tell if your daughter is becoming an SPG?

1. **If she starts wearing bare midriffs to church at 14.**
2. **If she opens her mouth wider than anybody else to sing the school song.**
3. **If she tries to tell you that her six-foot tall, 54-year-old oil rigger boyfriend is actually a St Patrick's boy.**
4. **If you find condoms taped to the bottom of her roller skates.**
5. **If she is picked up from school by an advertising executive driving a Jaguar.**
6. **If she enjoys being spanked by the teacher, and her teacher turns out to be a 45-year-old Australian film director.**
7. **If she starts going out with your maid every Sunday afternoon.**

WHITE CHRISTMAS *The ultimate SPG dream.*

There is no truth in the rumour that SPGs are school dropouts. Fact is, SPGs are very fast learners and apply their knowledge very strategically.

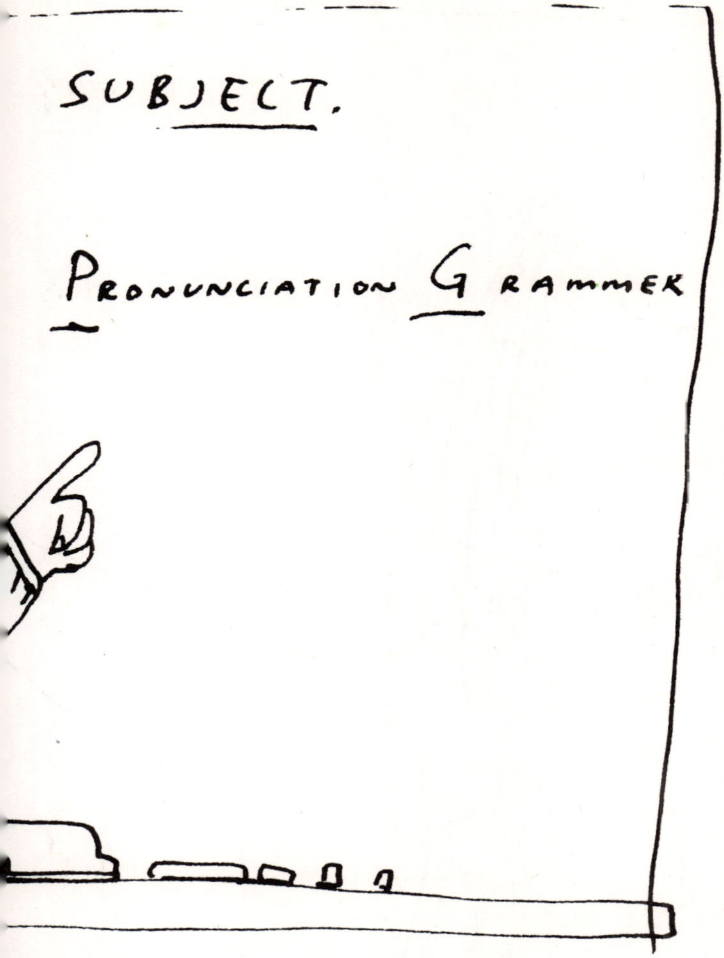

POPULAR BELIEF, SPG ARE

TAUGHT IN SCHOOLS.

SON, ARE YOU INTO NIRVANA OR SPG?

CHAPTER 6

THE SPG AT WORK

Far from being a brainless bimbo, airhead or space cadet, the SPG is an integral part of the Singapore economy. By day she slaves away in her chosen profession, only to find herself taking on an additional burden at night. For without her unstinting contribution, sales in the liquor, hotel and entertainment industries would fall by 35%.

Over 50% of all SPGs have either attended the National University of Singapore or know where to find it on a map.

Some have been under graduates, while

others were faculty members in Arts, Architecture and Law.

SPGs make loyal, dedicated workers, especially for white employers. SPGs are rarely found in Japanese-owned companies because they are usually twice the height of Japanese executives. Unlike their fellow Singaporean workers, SPGs are never on MC unless they are actually on an MC (Male Caucasian).

SPGs are often in demand because their English is very precise. Their vowels are extremely well rounded. For example, "Air Hair Lair" is the correct pronunciation of "Oh, hello". SPGs never use words like "lah" or "hoh" or "haw" or "loh" or "lei", in case they betrayed origins which they prefer to forget. The least used word in every SPG's vocabulary is "No".

The most popular word amongst SPGs is "lunge". It can often be heard in such statements as: "It's lungetime" or "Where are you taking me to lunge?" or "I'm going to lunge with the boss". As many white men have learned to their cost, there is no such thing as a Free Lunge.

SPGs can be counted upon to dress tastefully, albeit briefly. They regard expensive gold jewellery as very Chinak and never wear it. Another reason they never wear it is because white men never buy it for them. 95% of SPGs prefer simple ethnic pieces which stress their innocence and modesty.

While other Singaporeans complain about how cold the airconditioning is, the SPG is content. She will have achieved a very desirable state of nipple protrusion.

SPGs prefer to be driven to work. Bus travel is out because they find it difficult to manage the high steps in their shoes. Climbing into a bus when wearing an extra short mini-skirt can also lead to problems. Elderly passengers following behind can often mistake part of an SPG's anatomy for the ticket dispenser.

Once she starts work, the average SPG seeks the prestige of

A TYPICAL EXPAT ADVERTISING MAN (CREATIVE), SOMETIMES SPG SWOON OVER THEM, SOMETIMES NOT BECAUSE THEY LOOK POOR.

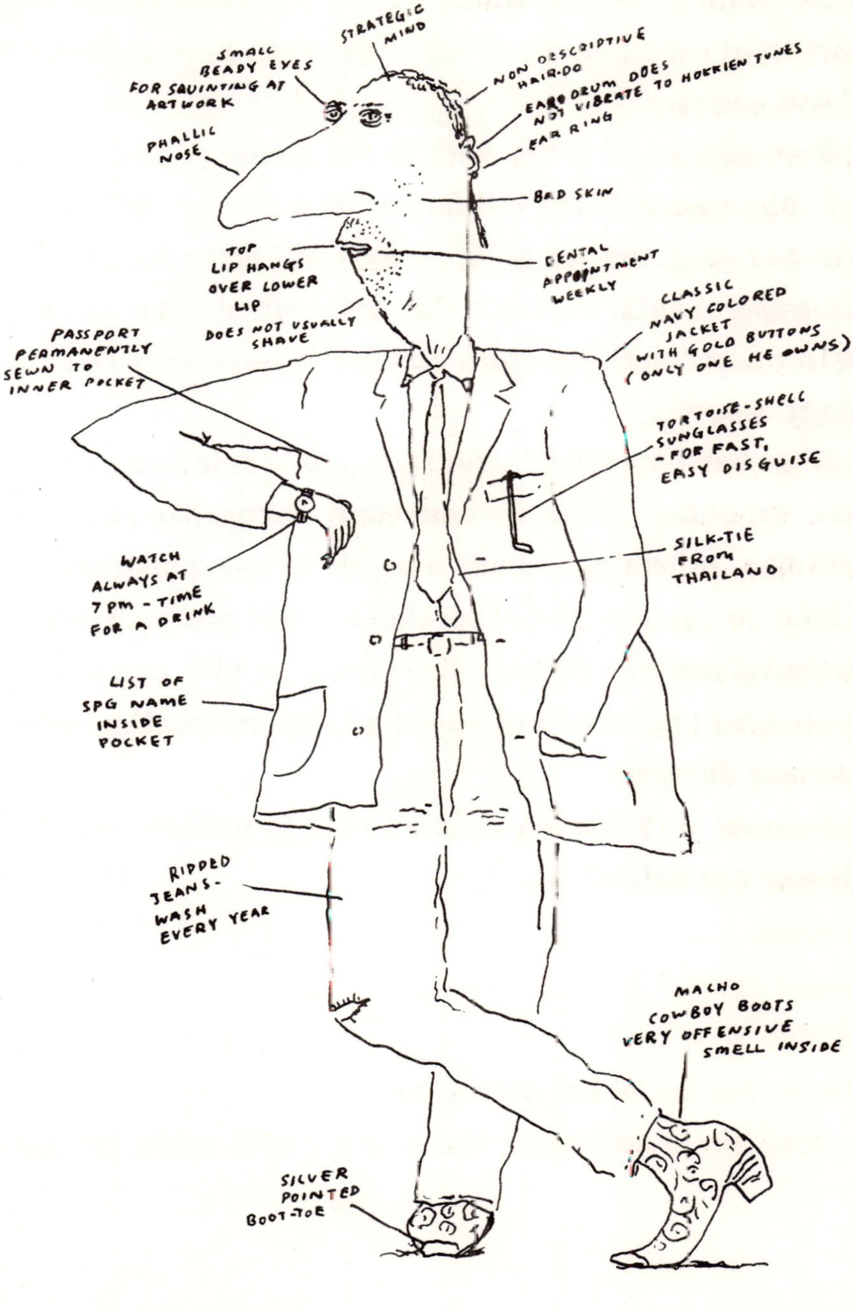

having an account with a foreign bank. Citibank will be her first choice, while POSB and OCBC will be regarded as too "local". (Apart from which, many SPGs might even have sisters who work in those banks.)

Over 60% of all SPGs work in the media.

A job in advertising will be her first choice. With her short skirts and long, tanned legs, an SPG will often be chosen to service the clients. Having a flat belly will also be an advantage. Expatriate account directors can use it when they're writing their contact reports.

SPGs have a natural talent for public relations, and the more public the better. SPGs are especially decorative at cocktail receptions, providing nobody asks them any questions.

Film companies and recording studios are a mecca for SPGs. By working her way through the ranks, an SPG can become a fully-fledged producer and spend all day on location with expatriate directors.

Because very few expatriates work in publishing, very few SPGs work in publishing.

SPG PRODUCERS SOMETIMES ARE A PAIN TO WORK WITH

DREAM OF EVERY SPG IS TO BE A SBC NEWSREADER

Many SPGs earn their livings as models. They are not required to speak or think, and they are ideal for fashion shows because they can undress faster than other women. Sadly, many SPG models have been accused of leading immoral lives. The truth is, the average SPG model is actually short-sighted so she doesn't know who she's with until they're almost on top of her.

Some SPGs often take up nursing. They see it as a noble calling which allows them to relieve their male patients.

There are no SPGs working in dental surgeries. SPGs think dentists are very strange people. She would never feel comfortable with a man who only wanted to put his fingers in her mouth.

More and more SPGs are now working as sales executives in real estate and insurance. In business, SPGs wear sleek jackets and short black skirts. Black stockings and black shoes are also essential. Her specially padded bras give her a prominent advantage over her more conventional colleagues. She will drink more, laugh louder and sleep later than anyone else on the staff. She can usually be distinguished by her perfect white teeth and scarlet lips. By her mid-twenties she will have developed child-bearing hips and a slightly bovine appearance. By her early thirties, her thighs will have become solid, muscular trunks and she will laugh like a rather

peculiar horse. As a result of eating too much rich food, her flat belly will have vanished and her shoulders will have become round. She may even be forced to sleep with a non-European customer occasionally.

Because SPGs have a flair for handling strangers, they often work as Guest Relations Officers in hotels. Slender SPGs in sober charcoal grey suits enjoy showing visitors everything Singapore has to offer. When they finish work at midnight there's still time to reach the bar and continue expanding their relations.

Upscale SPGs practise their subtle charms in the executive search industry. However, none of them were willing to tell us how many male executives they had found.

And, while it is highly unlikely that an SPG will ever become Prime Minister of Singapore, rumour has it that the SPGs have already formed a political party: the SDP, Sarong Democratic Party.

APPEARING ON TELEVISION IS A DREAM COME TRUE

Many SPGs believe they have artistic talents. And, of course, some actually do.

Expatriate men are usually deeply impressed by the sight of a creative young body.

Of course, some SPGs don't need to work. They have discovered many ingenious ways of separating a white man from his money.

For example, she can show him a photograph of a middle-aged oil-rigger and claim that:

1. She overlooked all his infidelities during five years of marriage.

2. He then deserted her and went back to Scotland.

3. Now she needs money for legal bills to enforce the maintenance payments for herself and their three children.

At which point the white man will give her $50 and jump into the first taxi he can find.

In special circumstances, however, she might ask for $200 and offer the following as collateral:

1. Her passport (the blue one, of course)

2. Her brother's passport (blue, preferably expired)

3. Her body.

THE ATTEMPT TO WRITE A BOOK WAS INDEED QUITE UNNERVING FOR THE AUTHORS

CHAPTER 7

THE SPG AT PLAY

Many SPGs become angry when they are classified as SPGs. They think of themselves as Women of the Nineties, the Jane Fondas and Madonnas of Singapore. And, like their icons, SPGs prefer a liberated lifestyle.

They enjoy watching ballet so they can discover a variety of interesting positions into which their supple, pliant bodies can be contorted in the bedroom.

Only 5% of all SPGs have ever attended a concert by the Singapore Symphony Orchestra, and only when persuaded to do so by a rich, intellectual expatriate. They find the sight of grown men blowing into horns vaguely disturbing. After attending an SSO concert, SPGs can fully appreciate why

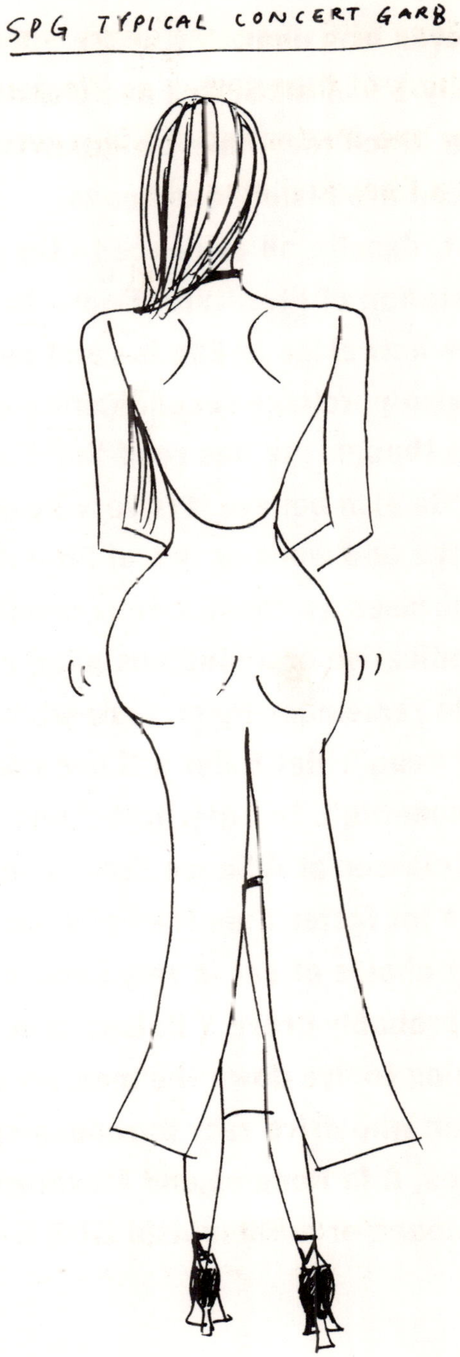

Beethoven was deaf.

Only 1% of all SPGs have visited a library after the age of sixteen. Once they have an expatriate boyfriend, the only books they read are his cheque books.

Yet, despite all evidence to the contrary, SPGs have a fine appreciation of literature. Books by Jackie Collins help them acquire new skills in English and new strategies for getting laid. SPGs also purchase secondhand books: they're cheap and they look as though she has read them many times.

SPGs also believe it is very fashionable and intellectual to throw the odd word or two of French into general conversation. Such phrases as "Voulez-vous couchez avec moi ce soir" are truly indicative of a studious mind and are well worth the hours it takes to remember them. Instead of eating chicken, she will devour "coq". Her toilet will become her "pissoir" or even "La maison merde". In order to achieve these linguistic feats, SPGs attend classes at Alliance Francaise, where they pick up the tutors a lot faster than they pick up the language.

Her choice of car is very important to the SPG psyche. Her father probably drove a Datsun Bluebird for ten years and she is still trying to live down the memory of it. She loves to be seen with men who drive racy European sports cars like Ferraris, Porsches, Alfa Romeos and Maseratis. She will however settle for an NX coupe or a Mitsubishi GTO.

SPGs are very hearty eaters. In fact, most SPGs will eat anything that is put in front of them.

Some SPGs have even been known to cook, so they will appear domesticated and suitable wife material. 99% of SPGs can fry an egg while wearing nothing except an apron.

To keep abreast of the news, SPGs read The New Paper. This is because they wake up too late to buy The Straits Times.

BANNED IN SINGAPORE, MADONNA'S
'SEX' BOOK IS SPG FAVOURITE BOOK
IT CONTAINS MATERIALS SO
HOT ITS WRAPPED IN A SILVER FOIL.
MOST SPG MIGHT OWN A COPY
SMUGGLED FROM ABROAD.

SPGs are often avid tennis players. Tennis provides many opportunities to show off their legs, breasts and panties, not necessarily in that order.

SPGs think it is very fashionable and trendy to go jogging. Jogging exercises every part of their bodies, especially when a bra isn't worn. Jogging SPGs are easily recognised by their gaudy sweatbands and extremely clean jogging shoes or bare feet.

SPGs are now taking an active interest in cricket and are frequently caught l.b.w. (leg behind whiteman). The padang (which is the Malay word for an open field) is a remarkably appropriate venue for them.

Few SPGs have taken up body building, as they don't enjoy being with men who have bigger breasts than them.

Throwing frisbees is a nice, undemanding pursuit for SPGs. In fact, SPGs can even be trained to catch frisbees in their mouths.

FOR A REFRESHING SUNDAY JOG

SPG JOGGING GEAR:

1) VERY THIN & SMALL SINGLET CUT OFF FOR MAXIMUM WAIST EXPOSURE.

2) VERY SHORT SHORTS FOR MAXIMUM BUM EXPOSURE

3) NO BRA

4) NO JOGGING SHOES

The average SPG is a firm believer in exercise.

However, she rarely goes to a gymnasium. She has severe doubts about men who regularly pump their bodies and the last thing she wants are muscles on her legs.

Aerobics are also a waste of time. She can see no point in putting on skimpy, body-hugging clothes just to bend over in front of other women.

Many SPGs are fascinated by horses.

Sometimes, rich expatriates invite SPGs to spend an afternoon at the races. She will sip champagne in a private box and smirk at all the contractors in the public stand.

If you laid two jockeys end to end, they would reach the height of an SPG. Whereas, if you laid two SPGs end to end, nobody would be surprised.

Horses don't mind SPGs either.

These days, many SPGs have discovered the joys of sailing. Scantily clad SPGs can be seen decorating many vessels for a weekend away on nearby island resorts.

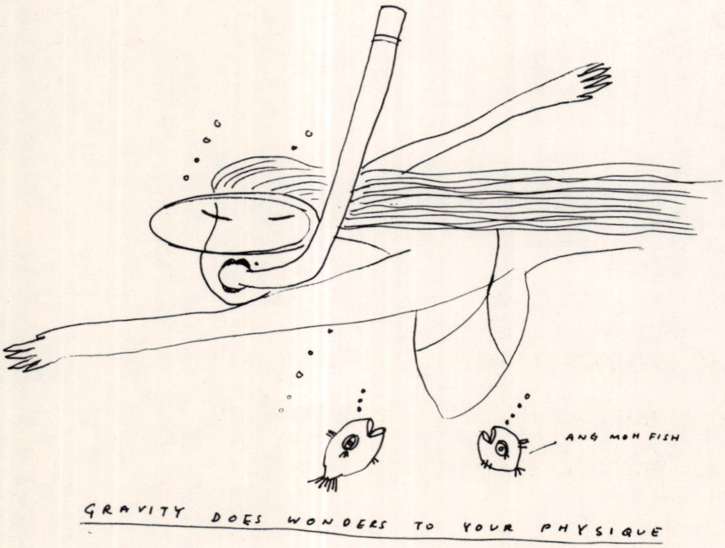

SPGs are remarkably adept at deep-sea diving, or any sport where they have to breathe in difficult or challenging circumstances.

PUBLIC WORKS DEPARTMENT *Responsible for the loose morals of SPGs by painting 'Hump Ahead' on Singapore's streets.*

91.5% of all SPGs journeying to Pulau Rawa appear to lose their bikini tops prior to arrival.

WWF
THE UNDERTAKER

SPG LOVE GOING ON SHORT TRIPS OVER THE WEEKEND. MOST OF THEIR PETS ARE LEFT AT HOME ALONE.

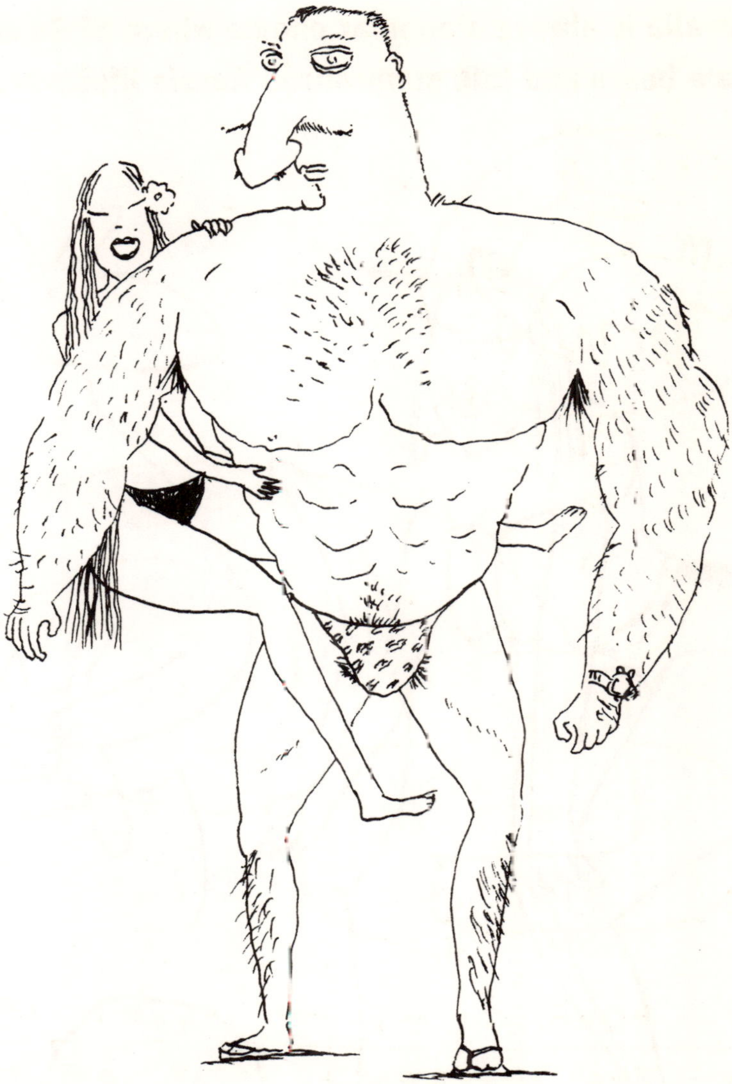

Generally speaking, SPGs are not fussy where they spend their holidays.

Australia is always a popular choice where SPGs can cuddle cute koala bears and tall, sunbronzed Aussie lifesavers.

SPGs would never dare to sunbathe topless on Bondi Beach as they would be overshadowed by their Australian counterparts. SPGs are frequently mistaken for Vietnamese Boat People.

However, SPGs soon adapt to life down under and pick up such useful phrases as "Owyergoinmate,orright?" and "Wotyergotyerhandsinmeknickersfor?"

An SPG's passport is always valid so she can accept any white man's invitation to travel anywhere in the world. Unfortunately, she doesn't realise that passports are not required for baggage.

SPGs might have very narrow hips, but they also have exceedingly broad horizons.

Any excuse to leave Singapore will seem perfectly reasonable.

However, the last place she will ever want to visit is Guilin!

I LÚRVE EVERYTHING ABOUT PAREÉ, IT ALSO HAVE THAT CERTAIN JENIS-SAY-KUA!
PARDONNE?

BUAH DADAH *A male Caucasian's favourite fruit.*

CHAPTER 8

PARTY TIME WITH THE SPG

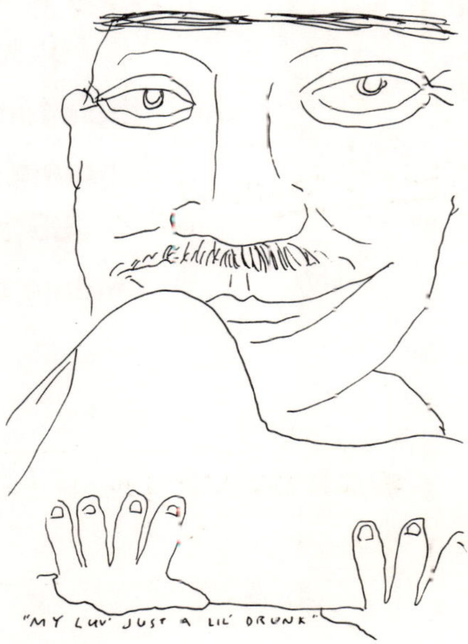

If you'd like to see the Sarong Party Girl in her natural habitat, may we suggest the following:

BRANNIGANS

99.9% of all SPGs have visited Brannigans at least once in the last week.

About the only thing they don't pick up at Brannigans is the bill.

SPGs do not object to the loud music. It saves them the mental anguish of having to make conversation. They also appreciate the height of the stools, allowing them to expose 54% more thigh than in any other bar.

91% of SPGs bring their toothbrushes to Brannigans.

95% also bring a change of underwear.

This is the aftermath of a bar visited by SPGs.

NUMBER 5

At Number 5, slightly older SPGs can be found sprinkled on nice, comfortable cushions. One of the regulars is a fat SPG called The Brick. Any expatriate sleeping with her will be called The Brick Layer.

USUAL SITTING POSITION AT THE CLUB

SOMETIMES, SPG HAVE IMPOSSIBLE DEMAND AT THE MOST UNLIKELY PLACES.

BABA LOUIE'S

A cozy bar in Erskine Road where long, lithe bodies are contorted over the snooker tables, baring their bottoms at the inebriated Australians hogging the bar.

HARD ROCK CAFE

SPGs wrongly believe this fabulous restaurant got its name because of the air-conditioning. SPGs wear low-cut tops without bras, so their nipples turn into hard rocks. While under the table, their white expatriate companions grow rock hard.

HARRY'S BAR

A discreet place to observe the nocturnal habits of SPGs who eat the free popcorn and listen to music they don't understand. A lot of SPGs go to Harry's because a lot of white men go to Harry's. Should an expatriate leave a tip for the waiter, the SPG usually manages to scoop it up on the way out.

WAITER, THERE IS AN SPG IN MY SOUP!

PONDEROSA

SPGs can often be seen with white male expatriates helping themselves to the salad buffet. However, given the length of her legs, it is not surprising that SPGs frequently end up with beetroot stains on their knees. Shorter customers in the queue behind them often think their rump steak has arrived.

BHAGRA NIGHTS AT DISCOS IS ONE OF SPG FAVOURITES

DELIFRANCE

An elegant, sophisticated rendezvous, much favoured by SPGs who like to be seen chewing long, crusty rolls while they pretend to read the French newspapers. Most of the time they manage to hold the pages the right way up. They also greatly admire French female singers who sound like they're singing with their mouths full. Because their hair is so long, SPGs automatically brush the bread crumbs off their chairs before they sit down. And, when they cross their legs, any remaining bread crumbs are cunningly concealed. SPGs go to Delifrance in the hope that, one day, they will find a Frenchman there.

BOAT QUAY

Hordes of SPGs in clinging black dresses can be observed nibbling on short, curly noodles and sipping copious white wines. Some SPGs sit precariously near the edge of the river in the hope they will fall in and be rescued by a passionate Italian waiter.

DRAWING INSPIRED BY A CERTAIN STOUT POSTER
SPG LOVE FRENCH LOAF IT GOES WELL WITH CHICKEN CURRY. ACCORDING TO A SPG FRIEND JASON & COLD STORAGE HAVE THE BEST FRENCH LOAF.

On the other hand, very few SPGs ever go to CLARKE QUAY, due to the proliferation of Japanese tourists and Ah Bengs.

SUNDOWNERS

An expatriate club where a ready supply of lonely white men is assured. A more intellectual type of SPG will be in attendance, usually stockbrokers, architects, lawyers and the odd advertising executive. These are the fringe SPGs, sporting sober dresses, horn-rimmed glasses and black stockings. Their brief cases will probably contain official documents, blueprints for condominiums, computer printouts

and lacy black underwear.

Of course, to really observe the SPG, one must go to a disco. Not that SPGs ever stand in the queues. Usually their provocative outfits ensure that elderly white men pay for their entrance immediately, after which the SPG quickly disappears into the crowd inside.

Her favourite nights are Tuesday (Ladies' Night at many discos), Friday and Saturday.

ZOUK

Mostly for teeny SPGs and Wanna-Be-SPGs, who cluster around the entrance waiting to be picked up by men who are older than their fathers. These SPGs are also known as Little Grunters or LBFMs, requiring frequent lubrication with Corona, tequila or vodka. They do not need to drink XO Beer in order to take it lying down.

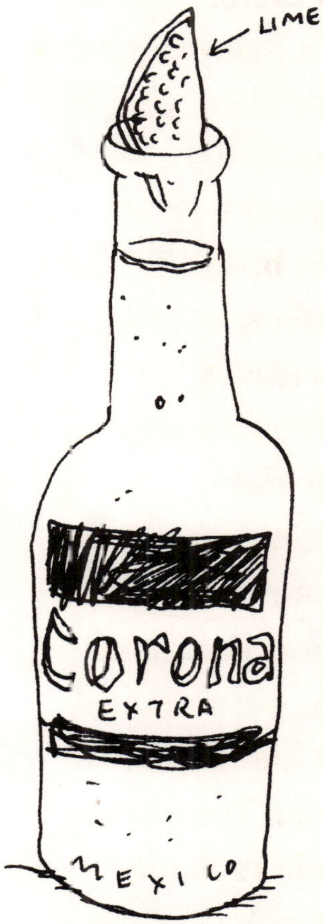

CORONA BEER FROM MEXICO. SPG'S HIPPEST DRINK WITH A WEDGE OF LIME. HAPPY HOURS

STUDEBAKERS

This is a very long and difficult word for the average SPG to remember. However, she will valiantly overcome all obstacles in order to follow the throng of glamourous, highly-paid expatriates who go there.

X'TRA / LARGE BOTTLE
WEDGE OF LIME
LIBERATED ARM POSITION
CORONA USED TO BE SPG HIPPEST BEER. IT PROBABLY STILL IS.
GUNG HO STANCE

GIRL, I'M GONNA MAKE YOU SWEAT
OH, YEH.

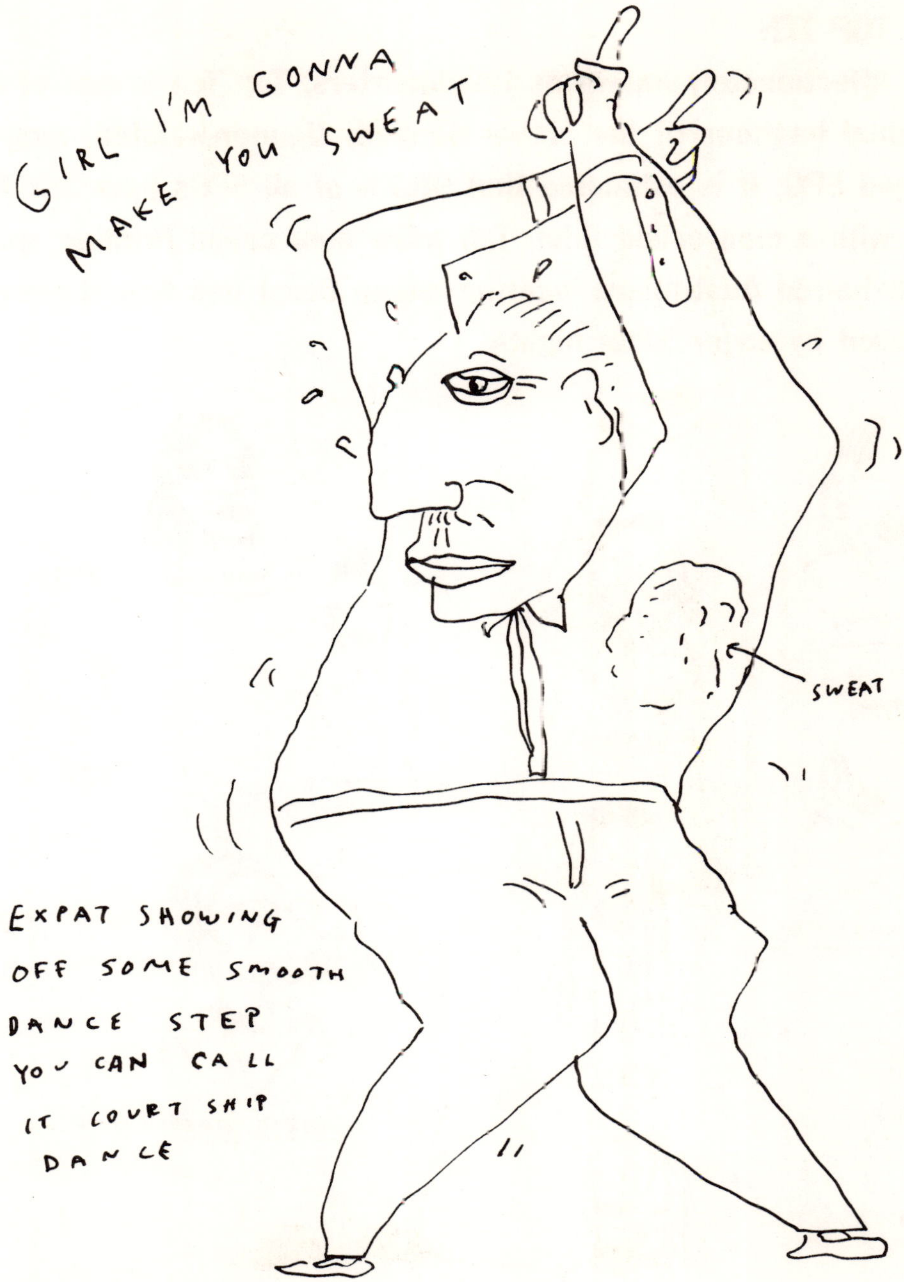
GIRL I'M GONNA MAKE YOU SWEAT
SWEAT
EXPAT SHOWING OFF SOME SMOOTH DANCE STEP YOU CAN CALL IT COURT SHIP DANCE

TOP TEN

Affectionately known as Headquarters, Top Ten is one of the original bastions of the brown-skinned, slender-waisted, long-legged SPG. It is estimated that 98.7% of all SPGs have left Top Ten with a man called John. Tall white men called Norman and curly-haired Australians wearing cheap floral ties find themselves mobbed by eager SPGs nightly.

Private parties in expatriate bungalows are also highly favoured by SPGs, with the older ones arriving in leopard skin tights to make them look more animalistic and wild. Poolside parties provide SPGs with the opportunity to fall in fully-clothed so she has an immediate excuse to disrobe.

SAUSAGES WAS FLYING ALL OVER THE PLACE AT THE BARBIE WHEN SPG ARRIVE

Barbies (short for barbecues) are social events popular with expatriate Australians and their SPG girl friends. SPGs need never go hungry because Australian cooks always keep a little pork in reserve.

One of Singapore's best kept secrets was Club Townerville, a terrace house in Towner Road which became the scene of wild advertising parties a few years ago. Naked men on motorcycles rode through the early morning streets, or cavorted with SPGs in a shallow wading pool on the balcony. Frequent fights with samurai swords and machetes continued well into the pre-dawn hours, culminating in the anointment of SPGs with salad oil.

SOMETIMES LOCALS MEANT WELL BUT OFTEN MISUNDERSTOOD

Not every single expatriate will look for female companionship in a disco or bar.

Sometimes old, retired SPGs work in massage parlours. It provides them with a little pocket money and a chance to keep their hand in.

MOST LOCALS LOVE KARAOKE, THEY TAKE THEMSELVES PRETTY SERIOUSLY. SPG COULDN'T UNDERSTAND WHY THEY CAN SING WITH A STRAIGHT FACE

CHAPTER 9

THE SPG AND SEX

SPG. Sexually Proficient Goddess.
She has become a caricature.
Admittedly of her own making, but then...

The SPG is the antithesis of Singapore's family values. She flies in the face of Singapore conventions.

Legends surround her sexual appetite. She is supposed to have a flat head, so a white man can rest his beer on it. And whereas other women have stretch marks on their stomachs, hers are around her mouth.

While most Asian women are wary of making love to a perfect stranger on their first date, an SPG is eager to learn just

how perfect he is.

Her definition of foreplay is having three or four drinks at Brannigans. And for her, heavy petting is an absolute waste of time.

Sex is her priority and marriage her hidden agenda.

Yet sadly, an SPG's hymen is something that's broken as quickly and easily as a white man's promise.

For the white man, the SPG is not a serious woman, more

his plaything, a brown fantasy in a tight black dress.

As far as a sex-hungry white man is concerned, she is on the same level as Whisky Tango, his code word for White Trash: those buxom, suntanned, hairy-legged Dutch and Belgian female backpackers who frequent cheap lodging houses along Beach Road and Bencoolen Street.

She is a Disposable Woman, and probably in many instances is oblivious to the fact.

But she will have her own distinct preferences, too.

For example, around 30% of SPGs would rather make love to a hairless white man. Another 50% prefer hairy men, in order to provide additional exercise for their fingers. (The other 20% have no opinions whatsoever, which isn't all that surprising.)

SPGs are quickly ignited by the sight of a well-proportioned male bottom. Her ideal specifications are:

1. Round, not oblong
2. Slightly protruding, so she can imagine it clenched in action
3. Not too thin (men with skinny buns are boys)
4. Not too fat (like her uncle's bum)
5. Smooth yet grippable
6. Sleek yet solidly reliable
7. White.

ANG MOH ALSO WEAR PERFUME
THEY OFTEN USE THOSE WITH MACHO NAMES.

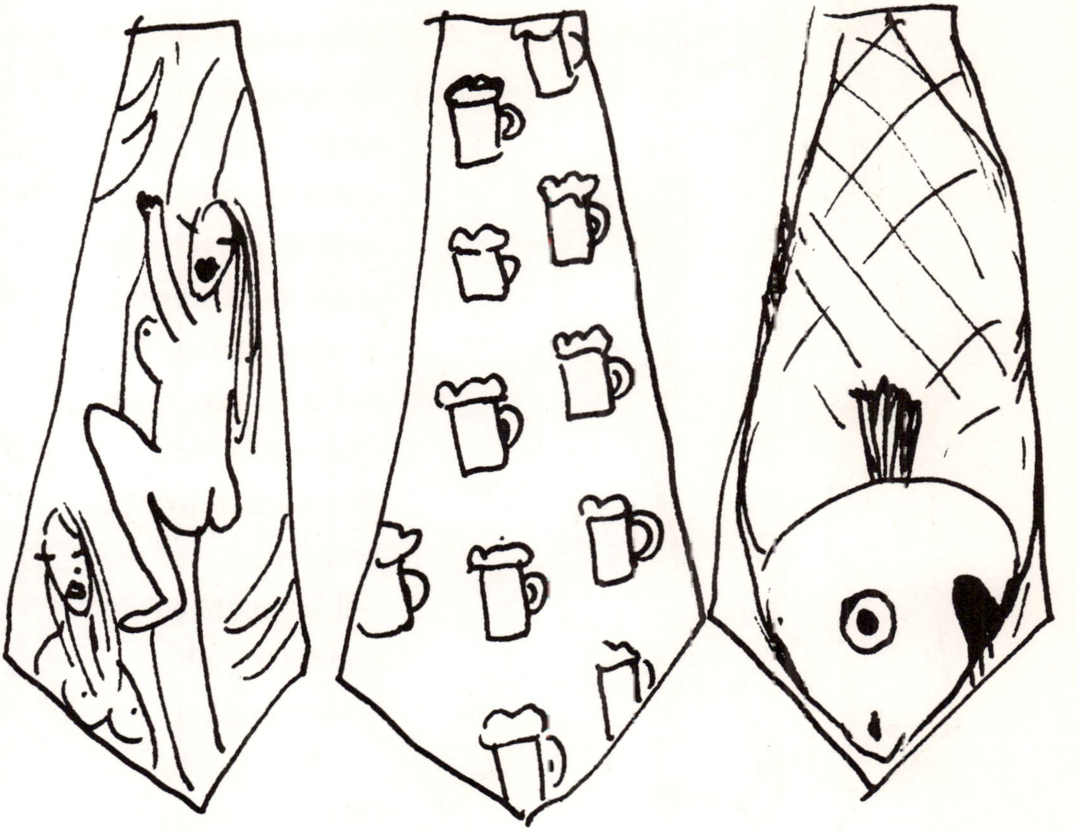

ANG MOHS' TIES TELL ALOT ABOUT THEIR LIKES OR DISLIKES - MOST OF THEM ARE PRETTY PREDICTABLE

A CRUEL SPG AT WORK

SPGs are strangely attracted to men who wear ties. A tie symbolises wealth and success, and an SPG likes nothing more than having a powerbroker in her bed. Any man who walks into Brannigans with a white shirt and tie will be mobbed by impressionable brown bimbos.

The fastest thing in Singapore is an SPG moving in to a white man's apartment. Districts 9, 10 and 11 are her favourite addresses. There are probably more SPGs per square inch in District 11 than any other part of Singapore. On Sunday morning, virtually every balcony boasts an SPG sunbathing topless.

CHAPTER 10

MARRIAGE AND AFTER MARRIAGE

SPG'S BABY - THEY'RE ALWAYS VERY CUTE BECAUSE OF MIXED BLOOD.

Courting an SPG is exceptionally easy.

A white man can tell her whatever he likes and she will believe him. She will swallow anything. On the other hand, she can resort to few tricks of her own...

Naturally she will insist on a white wedding in a church, much to the secret amusement of everyone who knows her. Half the congregation will comprise her old boyfriends who will idly wonder whatever happened to her sexy figure. (Some will even be ungracious enough to wonder what happened to the money they lent her five years ago.)

At the reception, her bridegroom will receive some amazing tips on how to keep her satisfied and the phrase "Best Man" will suddenly take on a new and horrific meaning.

By that time, of course, it will be too late for him to change his mind. And he'll probably be too old to care anyhow.

After marrying, 87% of SPGs revert to type and adopt the conservative social values of their parents. Her children will be given elegant and sophisticated English-sounding names.

SANDWICHES *Expatriate men love them, especially when an SPG is in the middle.*

DO YOU TAKE
THIS MAN...
I'LL TAKE
ANY MAN

As a service to expatriates, here is a list of SPG virgins:

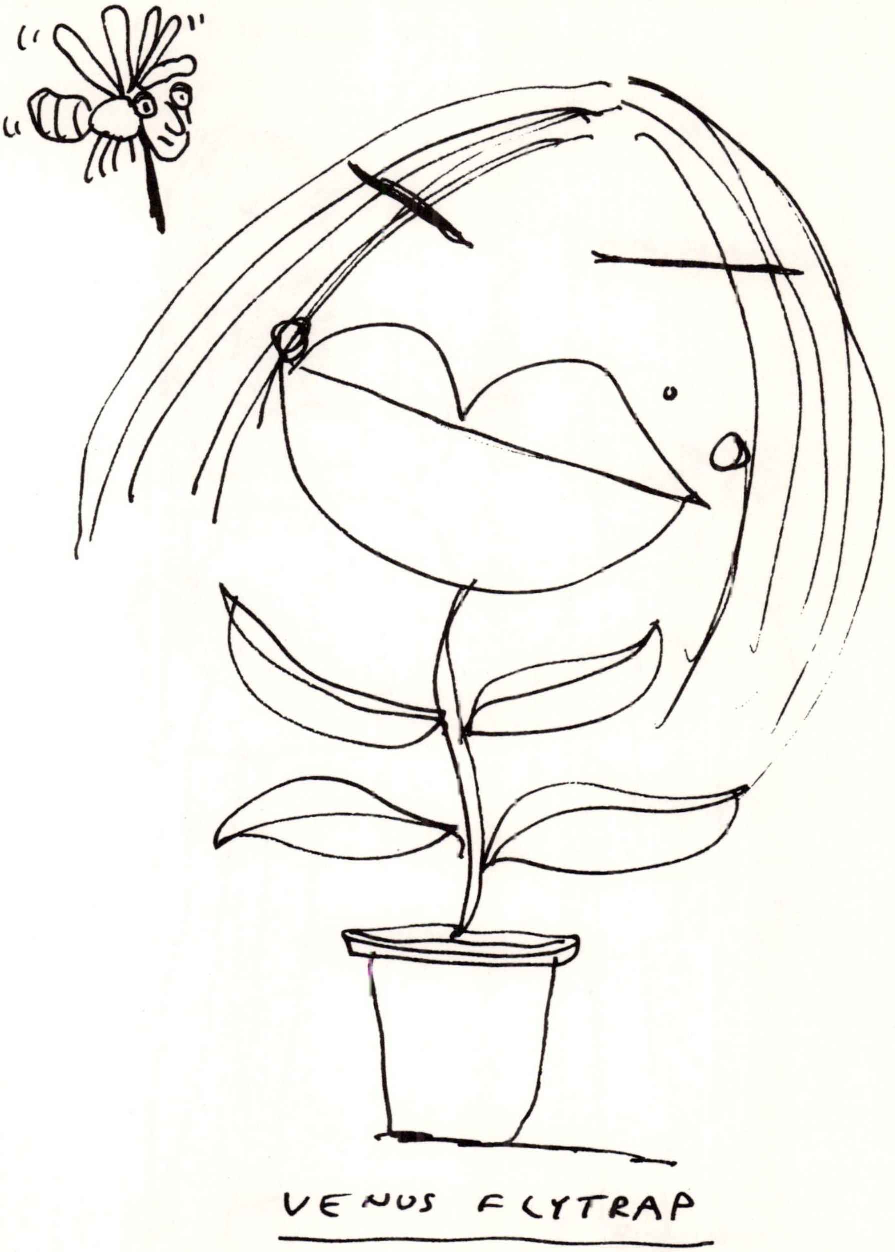

VENUS FLYTRAP

CAN YOU GET ME
A TAXI TO BRANNIGAN'S?
YES, MADAM!

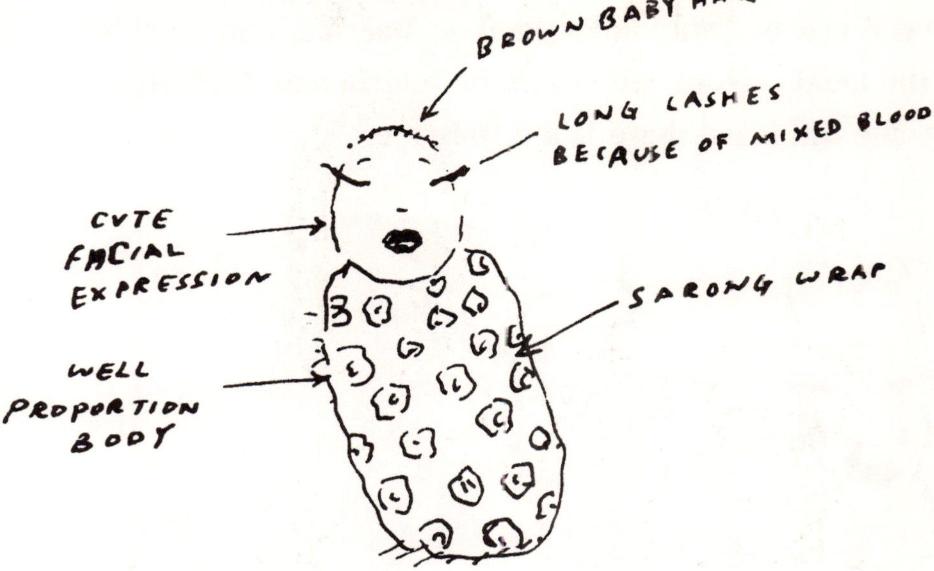

SPG's BABY

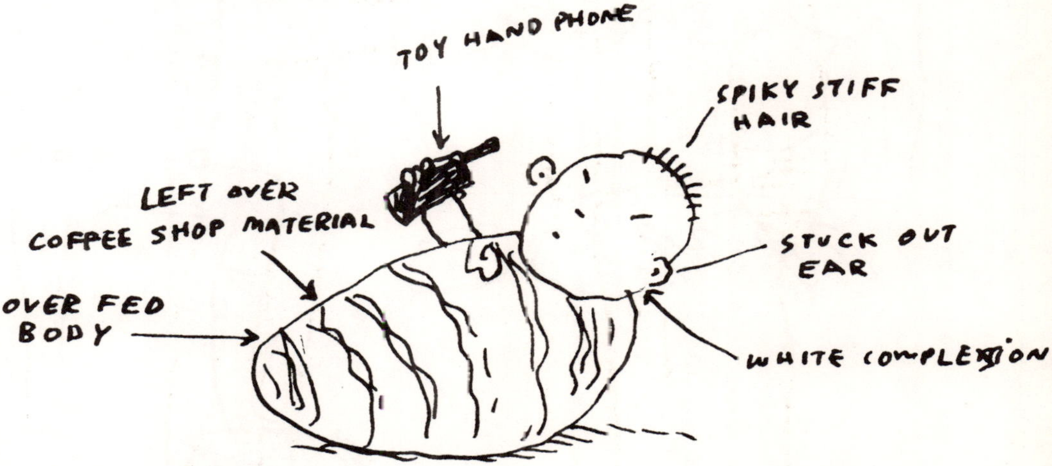

AH BENG'S BABY

Not all SPGs stay in Singapore once they get married.

Some will end up living in England or America, and quickly embrace the local culture. Others go to Austria and Australia; eventually she will learn there is a difference.

And if she finds herself living in New Zealand, life could be worse. At least she won't have to compete with other women: only sheep.

AND THEY LIVE HAPPILY EVER AFTER...

Occasionally though, old habits will reassert themselves and married SPGs will embark on nostalgic Nights On The Town, always in the company of other married SPGs. In the darkest corner of Scandals, and generally in the company of paunchy hotel executives, their flames will blaze briefly again.

Introducing the new...

SARONG PARTY DOLL!

● All models feature opening and closing mouths and legs.

● Complete with digital recording of sexy voice: "Oh John, I lerrrrrve you!"

● Pour alcohol into doll's mouth and she will fall over.

Full range of models include:

- Self-stripping bikini SPG doll.
- Auto exposing SPG doll. Teknologi baru!
- Black dress drops on spoken demand!
- SPG auto-slave, complete with automatically fluttering eyelids and built-in drool.
- College Queen. Complete with school uniform and books.
- OPTIONAL EXTRA Can teach you rude words in five dialects.
- TOP OF THE RANGE Little brown SPG with whip and nurse's uniform. ORANG PUTIH SPECIAL.

DON'T SEND MONEY!
She will only keep it.

Unjust? Or just plain vicious?

If you thought the SARONG PARTY GIRL was given a harsh treatment, don't worry: we're giving her the right of reply. Watch out for her book, REVENGE OF THE SPG, in which she puts expatriates under the microscope as well as under the sheets...